This book is written for those who care about youth, who see the plight of adolescent America and want to face head-on the plague of self-destruction. This book will help you understand the psyche of the young and hopeless, as well as provide you with the information and resources you need to reach out and help them.

SUICIDE:
KNOWING WHEN YOUR TEEN IS AT RISK

SUICIDE:
KNOWING WHEN YOUR TEEN IS AT RISK

"The best book on preventing suicide I have ever read. It took me behind the closed doors of teenage pain...and gave me workable, practical answers." **JIM BURNS**

T. MITCHEL ANTHONY

Regal Books
A Division of GL Publications
Ventura, California, U.S.A.

Published by Regal Books
A Division of GL Publications
Ventura, CA 93006
Printed in U.S.A.

Library of Congress Cataloging-in-Publication Data
  Anthony, T. Mitchel.
        Suicide : knowing when your teen is at risk / T. Mitchel
        Anthony.
              p. cm.
        ISBN 0-8307-1406-5
          1. Youth—United States—Suicidal behavior. 2. Suicide—United
              States—Prevention. I. Title.
  HV6546.A57 1991
  362.2'8'0835—dc20

                                                                91-9159
                                                                      CIP

The generic masculine pronoun is frequently used in this book to refer
equally to both male and female genders.

1 2 3 4 5 6 7 8 9 / KP / X3 / 95 94 93 92 91

Although the incidents in this book are real, all names have been changed.

Rights for publishing this book in other languages are contracted by
Gospel Literature International (GLINT) foundation. GLINT also pro-
vides technical help for the adaptation, translation, and publishing
of Bible study resources and books in scores of languages worldwide.
For further information, contact GLINT, Post Office Box 488,
Rosemead, California, 91770, U.S.A., or the publisher.

Contents

"Suicide could well be the most preventable form of death in our society today, if not in the history of the world."

"Suicide is happening because it is happening—it has become a self-propelling, self-destructive force."

"Suicide is not so much the desire to die as it is the fear of living."

"Compassion is paramount simply because all of the knowledge in the world cannot substitute for sincere concern."

Foreword

SUICIDE is something most of us have never had to contemplate or cope with in our own family—nor have we even been close to someone who has. We tend to almost dismiss it as "one of those things."

However, suicide is the number one plague among our American youth—along with alcohol and drugs. They all seem to go together—blurring statistics. Most Christians believe it is just a problem of the world's youth. Not so. The church statistics are growing.

Youth pastors should read and thoroughly understand this book. It depicts the real world and how to cope with it.

It was shocking one day in October of 1988 to discover that my next door neighbors' son was dead. He had broken up with his girlfriend and lost his job, all in the same week. He had accepted Christ but was put under great pressure from one of his disapproving parents.

If only he had talked to me, I thought. My heart was broken for him. He was a national-class triathlete and a hard worker. A fine boy, but all was lost.

A few months later I walked into a Christian's home in

San Antonio and was told their Christian son had just shot himself through the head. It turned out that a young female high school teacher had seduced him by coming to his home in the afternoon when his parents were gone. The school refused to even dismiss her (although she did leave). The 17-year-old boy was an all-league football star.

His parents knew something was wrong, but didn't know how to deal with it. This book can help parents to escape this tragic fate.

Fifteen-year-old Scott Garvey, an outstanding student and athlete from a happy home in Chicago, took his life in 1990, after taking a high high school English course on "Coping with Death and Dying." He left his book out so his parents could find it. It said, "Committing suicide may represent a last attempt to make an independent, personal decision."

Some of the activities in high school courses on death and dying have the students writing papers on "10 ways to commit suicide and select the best way"; "What would I do on my last day?"; "Write your own epitaph" and "Make out your death will." Other activities include taking a tour of a funeral home, lying in a casket and watching bodies being embalmed. Macabre to say the least.

Parents must become *aware*. Our 80,000 parents in Citizens for Excellence in Education (CEE)'s 500 chapters will welcome this tremendous book by one of America's most outstanding Christian youth authorities, Mitch Anthony.

We can finally know how to help the young, the hurting and the scared kids. Thank you, Mitch.

—Dr. Robert Simonds
President, Citizens for Excellence in Education
and the National Association of Christian Educators

Acknowledgments

Special Thanks...

To my typist, Debbie, for her persistence and indefatigable work ethic.

To my chief editor, Debbie, for her insight and ability to refine and purge a dross-filled script.

To my best friend, Debbie, for her encouragement and support.

And finally, to my wife, Debbie, for her loyalty and faith. This is our "baby."

Prologue

THE river below me was a familiar sight. I had spent my entire youth exploring its banks and its adjacent gardens. I also had rafted down its high, spring waters. By the light of the moon I could see the sharp, jagged rocks piercing through the surface of the water.

On this bridge, only a block from my home, I had often gathered my thoughts and pondered my life. This night was different, though. I was not standing on the bridge looking over the rail; rather, I was standing on the rail contemplating a headfirst leap.

I was 17 years old and searching. Although I came from a good home with loving parents, I was confused about life. Having recently lost a friend to death, I had been on a year-long quest to find some meaning in life.

During the recent weeks of sleepless nights, I had been stormed with questions I could not stop—nor answer. Being a fairly philosophical teenager, I wondered if life really meant anything. I came to the conclusion that it was some sort of theatrical event where people played certain roles, narrated certain lines and then exited the stage when their part was done. I was not sure life was something of which I wanted to be a part.

It was 2:30 A.M.—my moment of truth. I was contemplating a number of questions: What are you going to prove? Who is going to care a month from now? What if you don't die and you are maimed for life?

I don't know what kept me magnetized to the three-inch bridge rail, but the next thing I knew, I was waking up the following morning in my own bed. The only thing I had actually resolved was that I was not going to kill myself—at least for now. But it would not be the last time I would grapple with that notion.

I do not consider it ironic that my life has become one of offering hope to those whose lives parallel my own experience. I do not offer neat cliches or pat answers. I do, however, offer the fact that I understand how a young person can believe that suicide is the only path to take. I can say that I understand the inherent confusion of adolescence itself. How, coupled with the pain of indiscriminant tragedy and disappointment, it can seem emotionally and spiritually overwhelming. I can say that, in order to survive, we must learn to live with what we do not understand. And I can offer the fact that I am still here enjoying life simply because I have chosen to survive and do what I can to help others...that somehow, if we choose to, we can make it...that help can come to those who sincerely seek it.

For almost a decade I have crisscrossed the nation telling young people on junior high, high school and college campuses, as well as in churches and convention halls, that they are special and that there is purpose for them here on earth.

This book is written for those who care about youth, who

see the plight of adolescent America and want to face head-on the plague of self-destruction. This book will help you understand the psyche of the young and hopeless, as well as provide you with the information and resources you need to reach out and help them.

You just might find yourself crossing a bridge where another young man stands and wonders.

ONE
The Blackest of Plagues

If only...somehow
Why didn't I see
I cared so much?
Why didn't you call me
To give me a premonition
Of what you were to do
So I could prepare myself
To at least follow you?

Now I have only memories
And the cross you gave to me
That day and your sweet smile
Are remembered so clearly.

So many questions
Won't be answered today,
You're not here to ask
A gun took your voice away.[1]

These are the words of a teenage girl who lost her good friend to suicide—and in the process lost a part of herself. Her poem tells of the frustration and the confusion, the blanket of personal grief that normally follows a suicide. In this survivor's case, the tragedy plunged her into a depression so deep that she found herself battling the very killer she despised for taking her friend.

This is an intensely personal situation, but not uncommon. It is a scenario that we have seen repeated a thousand times. Only the faces and places and reasons are different. The result is always the same. One abbreviated life leaves behind a message of gloom to those still living. It renders them emotionally crippled, clawing, searching, groping for a thread of meaning not only in the death of their loved one but in their own existence as well.

LIVING VICTIMS

One by one the living victims of suicidal friends have come to tell me their stories of shattered worlds and dreams. They describe intensely painful days where minutes seem to stretch into infinity. No matter how many of these stories I hear, I feel a fresh sense of pain with each account. Each story is about a desperate person experiencing torturous pain. And worst of all, each story is true.

Although the names and scenarios differ greatly, there is always the same expression of pain engraved upon each face. I think of Tim, a high school senior, whom I met in a rap session with students who were contemplating suicide. Tim had the "greaser" look: straggly long brown hair, an attempt at a mustache, wearing a leather jacket. I could see that Tim was a nice-looking boy who was hiding his natural appeal behind an unkempt appearance. His distant eyes stared past me when I talked to him.

Tim had a hardness that belied his youth. His firm features revealed an intense, internal anger. He grudgingly and hesitantly answered my questions. When he finally opened up, he

---

Only God knows the impact suicide makes upon each human heart it touches and each life it disrupts.

---

stared at the wall as if his story was written on it and he was only reciting it. His emotionless tone of voice reminded me of the horror stories often told around the campfire.

The story Tim told was of his father's suicide five years previous. His father had put a shotgun to his own head when Tim was only 12 years old. As a result, Tim had spent the last five years in absolute inner solitude, trying to figure out why his father had killed himself. Now Tim is obsessed with thoughts of killing himself.

Then there is Becky, who came home to find her son, Steve, hanging limply in a noose in the upstairs hallway. Steve was only six days away from his birthday and his high school graduation day. He was intelligent and handsome, with many friends and a bright future—or so it seemed.

There is also Susan, whose ex-boyfriend told her that if she did not get back together with him, he was going to kill himself. She didn't. And he did.

Tracy is one I will never forget. Because of the unrelenting frustration they were feeling, he and his best friend Mike made a somewhat casual pact to kill themselves someday. I spent the day with Tracy the day after Mike shot himself. Tracy felt obligated to do the same because, in a way, he felt he had encouraged Mike to take his life.

And then there are Jim and Mary, who awoke one morning to find their lovely daughter charred to death in their driveway. In the middle of the night she had poured gasoline on herself and set herself on fire. What these survivors of the suicide of a loved one feel is painfully similar to what thousands of other fathers and mothers, brothers and sisters and friends have felt and continue to feel. The pain just does not seem to go away.

Only God knows the impact suicide makes upon each human heart it touches and each life it disrupts. We are only beginning to see the toll it takes. Each day hundreds of people in the United States are forced to experience the torture that comes with losing a loved one to suicide. These survivors of another's suicide are then at high risk of becoming suicide victims themselves. Hence, the chain of self-inflicted death continues.

THE UNKNOWN EPIDEMIC?

No clinics offer immunization or shelter for the plague of suicide. Judging from society's indifferent response, we might assume that suicide is not an immense problem. Even though we have been warned about the devastating effects of suicide, our response does not yet meet the need.

No group in our society has been insulated from this killer. For example, over 6,400 senior citizens kill themselves each year.[2] In addition, more than 60,000 Vietnam veterans have committed suicide since 1974—more than actually died in the Vietnam conflict.[3]

No group, however, has been so intimately affected by suicide as the teenage culture. Today's teenagers have been raised with a cultural ethic that condones self-destruction. We are living in a notably degenerate time in history, according to statistics relating to teenage difficulties. For example, the majority of teenagers have used alcohol and many have tried drugs.[4] As a result, drinking and driving accidents rival suicide as the leading cause of teenage deaths. In addition, sexual activity among teenagers is at an all-time high and the number of teenage pregnancies and cases of sexually transmitted diseases has increased. And more recently, the number of teenage crimes has increased significantly as a result of the current plague of occult involvement.

We would be hard-pressed to find a scourge in the history of our world to rival the modern one of teenage suicide. Like the Black Plague, the actual number of victims will never be known. Unlike the Black Plague, however, experts are *not* working around the clock to discover a cure. Yet suicide could well be the most preventable form of death in our society today, if not in the history of the world. My goal for this book is to present some conclusive evidence to support that claim.

Some half a million teenage suicide attempts are reported in the United States each year. But it is impossible to accurately calculate the actual number of victims because many suicides are not reported as such. The accuracy of statistics is affected by the social stigma of suicide.

For example, it would be impossible to prove that a sole-occupant car accident was a suicide, although it is not at all uncommon for teenagers to kill themselves in this way. Those determining the cause of death may want to spare a family the stigma, shame and confusion identified with suicide by simply reporting it as accidental or undetermined. In some cases, reports are falsified because of the possibility of a family losing a life insurance settlement as a result of a suicide determination. The same scenario is often played out in willful drug overdose deaths that are labeled accidental.

In some of these incidences, the "accidental death" determination is made even when a suicide note is found. It is much easier to give an erroneous death determination in a "marginal" suicide death where there is room for interpreta-

---

The difference between understanding and ignorance can be a matter of life and death for many promising young lives.

---

tion, whereas a gunshot to the head leaves little room for such an interpretation.

These reports then become the basis for the statistical reports on suicide. To illustrate, when Becky (mentioned earlier) found her son, the authorities asked if she would prefer "to have it written up as an accident." She was confused. She told me she understood that they were trying to protect her from the stigma of suicide but, she said, "I wondered if they thought it was going to change the reality of my pain."

Many families will deny an obvious suicide even in the face of indisputable evidence. The very idea of a loved one taking his or her own life is emotionally unpalatable. The denial process is complicated by the overwhelming sense of guilt and responsibility felt by the family. It is just too painful for family members to admit to each other that their loved one actually took his or her own life. Each member feels responsible for not preventing the loss. Hence, open admission of a suicide in a family is rare and, if it does occur, it is slow in coming.

The bottom line is that in recent years approximately 5,000 teenage suicides a year have been reported in the United States.[5] Many experts estimate that the actual number of suicides could be five to ten times as high as those reported. There is no scientific method by which we can discover the actual number of teenagers who have taken their lives. However, recent studies indicate a growing willingness among modern teenagers to entertain thoughts about how, when and why they might commit suicide.

It would be hard to overstate the current as well as the coming consequences of this suicidal trend if something is not done in every community to help abort it. This desperate situation will not change on its own. Other trends, such as the breakdown of the family unit and the decay of values and regard for life, "fuel the fire" of the suicide epidemic. These trends are not changing for the better, so we cannot expect the rampant suicide rate to subside, either. One thing is certain, with the number of teens attempting suicide every day we cannot afford to wait for these negative trends in society to correct themselves before we address the tragedy of suicide.

SUICIDE IS NOT THE PROBLEM

Because I personally contemplated suicide as a teenager, I know the feeling of wanting to die. Having been there has greatly influenced my perspective about suicide as a problem in our country. People are often startled when I tell them I do not believe that suicide is a *problem*. Instead, I believe it is a *symptom*—a symptom of problems, situations and trends that we have not recognized and dealt with properly. We are not dealing with a plague that defies remedy. The answers are readily available and simply await communication.

Whereas suicide is a symptom, the issues behind it are timeless: self-worth, faith, significance, purpose and the ability to cope with difficulty and disappointment. Part of the answer to the problem is to be found in a solid value structure: faith in God and self. If people are grounded spiritually, emotionally and psychologically, they are better equipped to survive adversity and hardship. Many of today's teenagers, however, do not have such a "grounding"—and many are not surviving.

A major stumbling block is that we live in a *reactive* society. Most people wait until the rope is around someone's neck to respond. What we really need is a *proactive* approach in which we prepare ahead of time for what might happen. For example, when a dinner guest is choking to death it is too late to learn the Heimlich maneuver. Similarly, we need an early warning approach to educate teenagers and those around teenagers on how to identify suicidal danger signs, how to respond to these signals properly and where to refer suicidal teenagers for help.

You don't have to be a professional to make a difference; every person reading this book can be a part of this proactive response and positive change. Most of all dissuaded suicides were done so by caring and concerned nonprofessionals.

WARNING SIGNS

Hopefully, all these precious lives lost to suicide were not lost in vain. As one mother who lost a daughter told me, "If my story and knowledge can help prevent this from happening to someone else, then maybe I can find some hint of significance in this." Tragedies such as those described in this book highlight the need to discover how and why suicides happen, how to see danger coming and, most importantly, how to stop these acts of self-destruction.

Knowing the warning signs or symptoms that may be displayed by a suicidal person is an essential first step. Explanations of the warning signs discussed in this book have been developed from true stories of what others have seen and heard before someone they loved ended his or her own life.

It is important that we not only *read* but also *heed* these indicators of danger to come. It may be a family member, friend, co-worker or casual acquaintance who first recognizes one of these ominous indicators. It is not important who identifies them but *that* someone recognizes these danger signals. The difference between understanding and ignorance can be a matter of life and death for many promising young lives.

Most loved ones who have lost a teenager to suicide say they never imagined it could happen to them, and that they did not see anything that would indicate that their loved one was experiencing any major problems. One reason for this is that many of the signs can be rather subtle. When common warning signs of suicide are described for survivors, many will recognize indicators that had preceded the suicide. At the time, however, they were not able to recognize behaviors or circumstances that might have hinted of an inclination toward suicide. Although they cannot be blamed, there is a lesson in this for all of us who are involved in the lives of teenagers: We need to be vigilant and sensitive to the conduct and conversation of teenagers. Following is an exploration of the early warning signs.

Talk of Suicide or Death
Meeting with Becky opened my eyes to the importance of listening to what people say during a troubled or depressed time in their lives. When she walked into my office, I was looking

into one of the most devastated and forlorn faces I had ever seen. There seemed to be a dark cloud hanging over her. As she started sharing her story with me, I began to understand why.

"I've got to do something—somehow—to help the cause of suicide prevention," Becky said. "It is the only way I can find any sense or purpose in Steve's death." She went on to tell how she had found her bright, handsome and personable son hanging in the upstairs hallway. I felt an unpleasant sensation in the pit of my stomach as she related her emotions regarding the tragedy. I was amazed that she even had the composure to talk without completely breaking down. Steve's death had even motivated her own failed suicide attempt.

"What hurts the most," she went on, "even more than losing Steve, is what I learned from his friends *after* his death. I began searching for any shred of evidence that someone might have had concerning Steve's mental state. I had no clue that something like this might happen. What I found out is just tearing me apart. Steve had told five of his friends that he was thinking of killing himself—and two of them were told *how!* Not one of them had bothered to come to me or to his father or anyone else to tell us what was going on."

Steve's death, like so many suicides, can be due partially to the ignorance of others of warning signs. Especially where teenagers are concerned, people can often fail to recognize a legitimate warning sign—even if it is as glaring as the noonday sun. Often teenagers do not take their friends seriously when they hear them talk of suicide. This may be due in part to the fact that teens often hear flippant, half-joking "suicidal innuendo" statements after a bad test, a bad game or other disappointing experiences: "I think I'll just kill myself" or "I can't take it anymore." Because many teenagers today frequently talk like this, it is difficult to distinguish a genuine statement of despondency from a superficial one.

In addition, because today's teenagers are exposed to an abundance of macabre and morbid language in film, music and literature, a friend's words about death do not evoke the reaction they should. Couple this with the fact that many people have been taught not to take talk of suicide seriously and you have a recipe for deadly negligence. Many cries for help simply go unnoticed.

Other Verbal Warning Signs

Verbal warning signs range from explicit statements of suicidal intention to implicit hints and even to bizarre and camouflaged insinuations. Popular belief to the contrary, the majority of those committing suicide have spoken of their intention. Previously unrecognized verbal warning signs are often identified in retrospect. *Explicit* verbal warning signs usually come in the form of statements such as:

- "I want to die."
- "I can't go on."
- "I wish I were dead."
- "I feel like killing myself."
- "I wish I were never born."
- "I can't take it anymore."

Such statements, as well as other similar dialogue, should be regarded as serious cries for help. Bear in mind that the individuals may not consciously realize that they are crying out for help. They may think they are just venting their frustration or expressing an emotion, when in actuality they are seeking an escape out of their pain or dilemma.

In many situations the verbal indicators are much more subtle, but no less serious. Examples of *implicit* verbal warning signs are statements such as:

- "You won't have to worry about me for long."
- "I won't be troubling you much longer."
- "Nothing matters."
- "I don't think I'll ever get that done" (spoken in a highly despondent tone).

All such statements could be regarded as ambiguous or having a double meaning. If a typical father heard his son say, "You won't have to worry about me for long," he might think, "Well, what do you know, maybe he is going to start acting more responsibly." Hence, the person's tone of voice or mood is an important indicator of the meaning behind the actual statement.

Finally, suicidal persons may verbalize strange or bizarre statements consisting of nebulous and nonsensical words. For example, a man in a rural setting told a friend and a relative that on the following Wednesday at 1 P.M. he was going to clean his gun in the barn. Both listeners were somewhat thrown off by the comment, but neither sensed the gravity of it and both failed to unravel the underlying message. At precisely 1 P.M. on the following Wednesday, the man put a shotgun under his chin and ended his life. Hidden in the strangeness and ambiguity of his comment was a desperate cry for help. Proud and self-reliant, he did not feel comfortable telling those close to him that he was troubled. Instead, he chose to disguise his anguish with a bizarre verbal clue in the hope that someone would pick up on it and respond. Sadly, no one did. I cannot help but believe that he wanted to live and that if anyone had shown up, even seconds before 1 P.M., his self-destructive act could have been averted.

I was once called into a high school the day after Mike, a popular athlete, had committed suicide. Upon hearing rumors that a suicide pact was forming, the principal called to see if

I would talk to those closest to the deceased. As is often the case after a suicide, a feeling of panic was in the air. School administrators were swamped with phone calls from nervous parents and with students who were unsettled and uneasy with grief.

In order to get to the bottom of the suicide pact rumors, I met first with the survivor that was the closest to Mike. I then met with the school's leadership to help form a strategy for dealing with the repercussions of this incident. What I learned during this day was illuminating and I will share much of it in a later chapter on the clustering of suicides. The most glaring discovery I made was that Mike's death was preceded by some rather unusual and striking verbal warning signs. For example, Mike's best friend, Tracy, informed me that on the day Mike killed himself he had uttered some troubling words to him. "When I was walking to my first class I ran into Mike. He had a strange sort of smirk on his face and he said, 'I've lost the fear!' That's all he said and he walked away."

I responded, "What did he mean by that, Tracy?"

"About two weeks ago Mike stayed overnight at my house and we stayed up late talking about things, you know, like life and girls and all that. Well, neither of us felt very good about the way life was going—especially with the girls we really liked. Then we started talking about suicide. We both decided that we would kind of like to do it, but we were too afraid of dying to try it. So when Mike said he had lost the fear, it started me worrying."

"Did he say anything else to you that day?" I inquired.

"Yes he did. And this was when I really got worried, but I just wasn't sure. Between first- and second-hour classes, he came up to me again. He had a glassy look in his eye and a sort of morbid tone in his voice when he said, 'I'll see you in hell, my friend!'"

At this point, I was mystified as to why Tracy had not responded to this obvious indicator. I asked, "Why didn't you go talk to someone at that point?"

Tracy quickly answered, "Mike was always joking around and I never quite knew when to take him serious. When he said, 'I'll see you in hell, my friend,' he was referring to the name of an album that we liked to listen to together.[6] So, I thought he might have been kidding around with me."

At this point, Tracy's voice began to break and his eyes pooled with tears. Still numb from the incident, he continued slowly, "I just sat there all day wondering what to do. In the afternoon I was sitting in a class and was jolted by the sound of a siren racing past the school, and I knew. I ran out of the school straight to Mike's house. When I got there, they were carrying him out on a stretcher—with a sheet covering his face."

This tragic story vividly illustrates the importance of keeping our ears open to verbal clues. By not taking his friend seriously, Tracy responded the way most teenagers would. Later, I will share about the profound effect Mike's death had upon Tracy. For now, I wish to highlight the fact that Mike gave verbal clues that were to some extent bizarre, but recognizable. He made statements that he knew would be meaningful to Tracy. Rather than giving a death notice, Mike was sending out a masked, but desperate cry for help.

No Laughing Matter
One of the reasons Tracy and his friends did not take Mike's words seriously was because they had heard this sort of talk from Mike before; they had become desensitized. But we see from Mike's story that joking around about serious matters can be a telltale sign. One mechanism many of us use to deal with uncomfortable subjects is to make light of them with

humorous statements. If someone tells an occasional joke about death, suicide or some other morbid theme, I would not be concerned. However, when I see that a person seems to have a humorous fixation on a morbid topic, the odds indicate that he or she is emotionally struggling with that particular issue.

Something I strongly emphasize for teenagers is to take their friends seriously. Having an alert and active sense of humor myself, I, too, look for opportunities to "lighten the air." I believe it is healthy to laugh. However, I also know what a camouflage humor can be for a troubled soul. Jokes can keep at bay anyone who might be seriously concerned about you. It is disarming to give others the false impression that everything is okay and that there is no need for concern. After all, if things were all that bad, would I be laughing?

A young girl once asked me, "How should I respond if my friend starts talking like that? I don't want to over-respond."

I suggested, "Imagine getting up in the morning and reading your friend's obituary in the newspaper. Then, ask yourself, 'What do I wish I had done?' Whatever you answer at that point is the course of action you should take—*now!* If you are wrong and that individual is not suicidal, you may be somewhat embarrassed—but he or she will know you care. If, however, you are right and do nothing, you could very well end up attending a funeral."

Any morbid preoccupation with themes such as death, terminal illness, graveyards, grief or even religious themes such as the Second Coming of Christ or life after death (not to be confused with the natural longing for Christ's return) may be indicators of an intention to commit suicide. Such fixations are not acquired at random. Usually they point to some underlying difficulty, pain or conflict.

Behavioral Warning Signs

During a discussion or rap session following a talk to a high school group, I was approached by a 17-year-old girl. In my talk she had heard me mention the giving away of valuable possessions as a late-stage behavioral warning sign. This prompted her to tell me about her ex-boyfriend who had recently lost his mother to cancer.

"Last week he gave away his deceased mother's wedding ring. At the time we thought it was a little strange, but we did not realize it was a danger signal. What do you think I should do?" she asked.

"You've already done the right thing by coming forward to talk about it," I assured her. "We need to go talk to the principal about this. Are you willing to tell him what you just told me?"

After agreeing she would, we went to see the principal. It so happened that the high school principal knew the boy's father fairly well. After talking about how to discuss the matter with the father, the principal called him. The father intervened with his son and learned that his son not only was seriously contemplating suicide but had also chosen a method and a time. The young girl's courageous decision to come forward with what she knew, could very well have saved his life.

The giving away of valuable possessions is regarded as one of the most radical behavior signals and should be responded to immediately. Any other *final-arrangement-type behavior*, such as making out a will or sudden reconciliation with long-time enemies, should be taken as a clear indication of preparation for death.

Another behavioral warning sign is growing depression and despondency reflected in the daily habits of an individual. If there are obvious changes in habits and behavior, we can safely assume that there is some degree of emotional disturbance. There are six general areas which should be watched for identifiable changes:

- *Eating*—eating too little or too much resulting in drastic weight gain or noticeable weight loss;
- *Sleeping*—sleeping much longer than usual or developing patterns of insomnia. The symptoms of either extreme can be persistent fatigue or hyperactivity and restlessness;
- *Grooming*—disintegration in appearance relative to the person's normal grooming habits. A disheveled and sloppy appearance can be a sign of depression and a way of saying, "I no longer care about me";
- *Social Activity*—depressed or troubled individuals normally become increasingly withdrawn. They may retreat from usual activities or interests, isolating themselves to only one friend or no friends. These individuals may become uncommunicative, unenthusiastic and gloomy. In addition, it is important to watch their ability to hold onto friends and maintain social relationships. The higher the degree of social isolation, the higher risk the person is.
- *Personality Changes*—a normally mild, independent type of individual often becomes loud, angry, hostile and even violent. On the other hand, a normally outgoing, sociable individual often grows reclusive and overly introspective.

Alert observation and intervention will often break down the defenses of those teenagers who are doing their best to camouflage their hurt and despondency. If you are well acquainted with a person, and he or she seems more intense or frivolous than normal, it could be a sign of trying to cover up an internal struggle. Making solid eye contact with this type of person can often unveil his or her true inner state. Because of a dark and troubled look in a teenager's eyes, I have often persisted in trying to uncover what is troubling him or her. Consequently, I have often found that the individual's situation is much more serious than was initially revealed.

Following a long gloomy period, suicidal individuals often display a *sudden euphoria*. The logic behind this is that internally they feel they have resolved their turmoil and conflict by resting on the "solution," namely, suicide. A person suffering a great degree of inner pain and turbulence with no end in sight can often be duped by a sudden sense of resolution of their circumstances. Friends and family members are fooled by a suicidal teen's apparent demeanor of happiness when, in fact, they are now at one of the highest levels of risk for suicide. When this state of peaceful contemplation occurs, the individual should be responded to immediately.

Situational Warning Signs

Most of the young people who attempt suicide today come from broken homes. Of the remaining young suicide attempters, many are living in turbulent family situations. It is critical to look at the domestic situation, as well as the recent events and history of a young person whom you suspect of being suicidal. Doing this will allow you to correctly assess his or her actual risk level. Any teenager who has displayed verbal or behavioral indicators and fits any of the following descriptions must be regarded as extremely high risk. Some *situational warning signs* are:

- Those who are socially isolated, have no friends or have trouble maintaining friendships;

- Those who have experienced drug and/or alcohol abuse either in their family or their own lives;
- Those who have been or are being abused physically, sexually or verbally;
- Those teenagers who are not living at home;
- Those who have had or are facing a significant loss: death of a loved one, divorce, the breakup of a romantic relationship, loss of financial or social status, family bankruptcy or foreclosure (note that the anniversaries of these losses are high risk periods);
- Those who are firstborn of either sex. Firstborn children often feel a pressure to set an example and to always do right; .
- Those with a history of psychiatric disorders;
- Those who have previously attempted suicide. Four out of five young people who kill themselves this year will have attempted suicide before (we do not always know of every attempt that has taken place). Approximately 12 percent of adolescents who attempt suicide this year will successfully complete it within the next two years;[7]
- Survivors of suicide are much more likely to take their own life. This explanation is given in Rita Robinson's Book *Survivors of Suicide.*

    "Many survivors of suicide report that they feared they might take their own life following the suicide of a loved one. There seemd to be obvious reasons for this, although many factors may be involved. The first is simply that suicide has been added to their frame of reference...second they may be generally susceptible to depression, mental and emotional instability...finally they are depressed about their loved one's suicide."[8]
- A sign that is often unnoticed on the typical warning sign lists are those teenagers who are highly perfection-

istic and self-critical. This indicator appears most often among sharp, intellectual, articulate and high-achieving types of individuals. Despite the outward successes and popularity of these teenagers they often feel that life is unsatisfying. They feel they are not meeting their own perfectionistic standards and expectations.

What I have given you here is a fairly comprehensive description of what to watch for in the conversation, behavior, life-style, history and current events in the life of a teenager. I cannot overemphasize the importance of serious regard for each danger signal I have mentioned.

To conclude, I want to relay the words Becky shared with me after losing her son, Steve: "Mitch, as you travel and speak, please tell people to take their friends and sons and daughters seriously. I can't bring Steve back, but maybe my story can help to spare another mother the hell I live with every day."

I think Becky is right.

Notes

1. Anonymous.
2. J. L. McIntosh, *U. S. Suicide: 1987 Official Final Data* (Hyattsville, MD: National Center for Health Statistics, 1987), p.1.
3. Many experts agree with this finding although it is officially denied by the Veterans Administration.
4. "The Patterns of Abuse," *Newsweek* (Summer/Fall, 1990), p. 59, quoting the University of Michigan.
5. J. L. McIntosh, *U. S. Suicide: 1987 Official Final Data* (Hyattsville, MD: National Center for Health Statistics, 1987), p.1.
6. Grim Reaper, "See You in Hell," from the album titled *See You in Hell* (RCA Records, 1984).
7. Phi Delta Kappa Task Force on Adolescent Suicide Staff, *Responding to Adolescent Suicide* (Bloomington, IN: Phi Delta Kappa, 1988).
8. Rita Robinson, *Survivors of Suicide* (San Bernardino, CA: The Borgo Press, 1989), pp. 100-101.

Two

I Just Want to Know Why

WITH his hit song of the 1970s, Paul McCartney made popular the axiom, "Live and let die." He was reflecting the growing attitude that seemed to say, "You do your own thing and I'll do mine." Few of us realized the toll that attitude would take on our culture.

Sitting among groups of survivors of suicide (those left behind by suicide), I continually hear the statement, "I just want to know why. I can get some rest and be at peace with this death if I can just know why it happened." Society is asking the same question concerning the suicide epidemic we are facing.

Our society wants a neat, concise explanation for each

malady it encounters. An autopsy can reveal the physiological cause of death—cancer and other fatal diseases. In addition, most fatal accidents provide a fairly tidy explanation for what caused the death—a teenager dies as a result of driving while intoxicated.

But in the obvious suicide death, loved ones and society demand a deeper definition of cause. It is not enough to say

---

Within the last 30 years ethical standards concerning respect for life and the importance of family preservation have rapidly disintegrated.

---

that John Q. Despondent's death was caused by a self-inflicted gunshot wound to the head. People want to know *why* he put a gun to his head and pulled the trigger.

Yet, I want to know why society is not asking the same question about the teenager killed in a drinking-and-driving accident. That young person died, in physical terms, from the result of a crash; however, there may be a deeper, psychological and emotional explanation for what happened. For example, the root causes may have been carelessness, negligence, an attitude of teenage indestructibility or rebellion. These causes point heavily to a self-destructive tendency in the young person.

This social mind-set makes it expedient for me to avoid writing a chapter that lists a tight, comprehensive list of causes of death by suicide. The causes for each suicide are a unique combination of factors, stresses and traumas rather than a single factor. Most of the traumas and stresses that teenagers today are ill-equipped to deal with have been in existence for ages. They include family problems, false expectations, the unpredictable changes of life, and a feeling of alienation from God's love and purpose in their lives. The result of this has been that the great ethic of respect for life itself has changed. For example, a Christian would be strongly dissuaded from self-destruction because of the hope offered in 1 Cor. 10:13. God's promise states that He will not allow anything to come into our lives that we can not overcome with His help.

The principle factor that *has* changed in recent years is the ethic about life itself. By this I mean the great respect people once had for life, the persistence and forbearance with which people once faced trouble and the consideration of ways personal actions affect others.

SHIFTS IN SOCIETY

Before talking about the cultural encouragements toward suicide that teenagers receive, it is essential that we discuss the factors that make them vulnerable to this message of destruction.

Disintegrating Values

Suicide has always been a fact of life and death; this is evident even in ancient literature. However, the increasing incidence of suicide that our modern society has witnessed is unprecedented. To understand the forces behind the current suicide epidemic, we must closely examine the degeneration of our society's social, cultural, philosophical and ethical standards. For example, within the last 30 years ethical standards concerning respect for life and the importance of family preservation have rapidly disintegrated.

Many social observers would claim that the changes I refer to as *regressive* are, in fact, *progressive*. However, those who feel these changes are progressive are hard-pressed to explain the overwhelming rise in social irresponsibility and in destructive and self-destructive behavior. Those who feel that the changes in society are neither regressive nor progressive are like a painter trying to blend black and white to form a pleasant, cheerful grey. They succeed only in polluting the white and denying the strength of the black.

Our public educational system has become hypersensitive to words such as "spiritual" and "moral"; for this reason I emphasize the word "ethical." What society doesn't recognize is that all the great religions and most of the political systems of our world, Eastern as well as Western, have as their foundation an ethic that declares respect for human life. In such systems it is not necessary to preach that human life has value and purpose. Neither does one have to define a redemptive plan, describe an eternal abode or even post a list of commandments in order to implant the necessary ethics for the survival and preservation of that society. Yet these ethics seem to have all but disappeared. By avoiding any form of education beyond the intellectual realm, many in our society have failed to receive any education in the ethical, spiritual realms. Professor Allan Bloom from the University of Chicago articulated this educational dilemma in his book, *The Closing of the American Mind*. He noted the prominent rise of a "new language of value relativism" which effectively prevents us from:

> Talking with any conviction about good and evil. The great classics of philosophy, history and literature were once studied to help find answers to the meaning of life and to illuminate the struggle between right and wrong. Now, if they are offered, they are treated as trivial enhancements to one's life-style. Some professors skip over any embarrassing preoccupation with "eternal ver-

ities," apologize for their "sexism" and bring them "up to date" with the latest psychological interpretations. The eternal conflict between good and evil has been replaced with "I'm okay, you're okay." Men and women once paid for difficult choices with their reputations, their sanity, even their lives. But no more, "America today has no-fault automobile accidents, no-fault divorces, and it is moving with the aid of modern philosophy toward no-fault choices."[1]

So, who is to blame? I have yet to see a suicide take place without the bereaved either absorbing the blame or placing the blame on someone else. However, can one person be blamed for another's life or death action? If not, where then does the fault lie? I believe it lies primarily upon a faulty ideological foundation.

As one can hardly deny, ethical standards among adolescents have been declining. The modern standards of ideas and principles by which adolescents are basing their lives are moving toward narcissism and nihilism. Ten years ago I was concerned about the apathy in our society; today I believe that apathy is being challenged by antipathy. Possibly worse than an "I don't care" attitude is the attitude that says, "I don't care about those who do." For example, while in an elevator I noticed a phrase on a young man's T-shirt which expressed his philosophy: "Excuse me, you must have mistaken me for someone who gives a _____."

The children of narcissism are concerned with how they look. They believe only in themselves; they worship themselves; they serve themselves. On the other hand, the children of nihilism believe in nothing. They venerate nothing; they serve nothing. Professor Bloom addresses this when he writes:

Students have powerful images of what a perfect body is and pursue it incessantly. But deprived of literary guidance, they no longer have any image of a perfect soul and hence do not long to have one. Asked what books they most enjoy or admire, students are silent, puzzled by the question. The notion of books as companions is foreign to them.[2]

These philosophies of life are beginning to take their toll on young people. At a pace of over 1,300 per day,[3] many of the children of the "live and let die" and "do your own thing" heritage are destroying themselves with drugs, alcohol and suicide attempts. What will their children add to our society?

I have asked thousands of teenagers what they believe in and have heard the same replies hundreds of times: "nothing" or "me" or "money." "Me" and "money" are the fruits of narcissism, whereas "nothing" is the evidence of nihilism. Subsequently, the issue that must be dealt with is not the struggles teenagers are facing but their attitude toward the purpose and significance of life. The glory of narcissism will fade with the first signs of physical decay and the satisfaction of nihilism will result in the despair of feeling that there is nothing worthwhile in life.

Any attempt to encourage such a young person to continue living in the face of trouble, perplexity and pressure is futile until these ideologies are challenged. For example, a church worker faced with these empty ideologies finds the ideal opportunity to present Jesus Christ's claim, "I am come that they may have life, and that they might have it more abundantly" (John 10:10, *KJV*), and to challenge the hopeless individual to test this claim for himself or herself.

We must remember, however, that the blame does not rest

solely on the teenagers; their beliefs and attitudes have been learned from home and society. Many of these young people have seen self-interest and self-indulgence serve as the main criteria for decision-making. Many also have seen their family units severed, materialism worshiped and their minds bombarded with the message that "looking good and feeling good" are more important than "being good."

Of course, the example of the perfect soul mentioned by Bloom does exist in the Gospels. Jesus Christ's tenderness, benevolence and compassion are a model for believers. Paul exhorted the early believers to "Follow my example, as I follow the example of Christ" (1 Cor. 11:1). Young people today have no greater need than that of a spiritual model—both in the seen and unseen realms. Young people need not only to see Christ's example as depicted in the Bible, but to see those around them physically living out that example.

Some members of society point an accusing finger at teenage culture as the reason for self-destructive behavior among modern teenagers. They blame teenage music, games and movies. However, this convenient explanation "strains at the gnat and swallows the camel." Even if we were to purge our society of every irresponsible, rebellious and destructive recording, band, book, game, television show and movie, the ideologies that stimulated their production would surface again in some other form and continue to press young people toward suicide.

The Breakdown of the Family

For the last 30 years sociological trends show a strong correlation between the rising teen suicide rate and divorce. One such study was conducted by Steven Stack, a Pennsylvania State University sociologist who identified the major sociological predictors of teen suicide. The study demonstrated that during the years when the divorce rate dipped slightly, the teenage suicide rate also dropped.[4]

In addition, most teenage suicides happen among adolescents from broken homes. I asked a social worker, who conducts support groups for teenagers whose parents were either divorced or in the process of being divorced, if she felt there was a relationship between the child from a divorced home and a tendency toward self-destructive behavior. She remarked that most of the adolescents she counsels have blamed themselves for the separation or divorce of their parents.

In some instances, this is due to one parent placing blame for the divorce on the offspring. In most situations, however, self-blame is due to the child believing that he or she had the power to positively or negatively control the situation. For example, a child may think, "If I hadn't acted that way, they would have stayed together." In other cases, the troubled teenagers stated that their parents would be happily married if they were out of the picture. The problem of self-blame must be addressed repeatedly; too many children are convinced of it and are suffering needlessly.

The Self-blame Phenomenon
This is not to infer that simply because a family has experienced a divorce that the children are an immediate risk for suicide. It is to suggest that self-blaming thought patterns could act as a strong *precipitator* toward the *potential* contemplation of suicide. Parents who have gone through a divorce do not need any unnecessary burden of pain or guilt heaped upon them. But they do need to be sensitive to the emotional ramifications and realities that their children are facing as a result of the divorce. This self-blaming phenomenon is but one example of how the breakdown of the family unit has contributed to the growth of a self-destructive ethic in teenagers today.

Why society is facing such a crisis on the home front is a complicated question. Yet it is clear that the more separation and severance children see and experience, the more hopeless and despondent their own outlook on life may become. It is also apparent that the breakdown of the family unit is related closely to the ethical disintegration of recent decades. The problem does not lie solely with the ethics held by a man and a woman, but also with the ethics of society as a whole as expressed in the marriage commitment.

The ethical breakdown concerning family, by and large, is the result of individual and corporate spiritual bankruptcy. From the Ten Commandments to the Sermon on the Mount, most of the positive ethics in our society are spiritually inspired, or "God-breathed." The fact that family ethics are breaking down is secondary to the fact that many people have quit looking to God for guidance and accountability.

The Ethics Factor

For example, I found it interesting to hear a comparison of the ethics of a friend who practiced law some 50 years ago and those held by many attorneys today. My friend, Harold Lincoln, entered his profession as a lawyer then went on to become a law professor and then worked in the U.S. Justice Department in Washington, D.C. during the Kennedy administration.

One night as my brother and I were having dinner with Harold and his wife, Evelyn, the topic of the modern lawyer came up. "When I was a young lawyer," Harold informed us, "we almost starved." He looked at his wife, Evelyn, who nodded affirmatively, punctuating his statement.

"Why is that?" I offered, sensing that Harold wanted to continue his line of thought.

"Well," he said, "when I first became a lawyer and first

hung out my shingle, the only people that came to me for legal help were those seeking a divorce. My policy was to first do everything within my power to direct that person toward reconciliation. So, I would ask the person to bring his mate to the next appointment. The next time the couple came in, you could sense their uneasiness. I would begin to query them about how their relationship began, what attracted them to one another, why they had decided to get married, how they had made it as long as they did, etc.

"Sometimes," Harold continued, "when I asked them how the trouble had begun, they couldn't answer. They had difficulty tracing the source. Do you know," he said with a grin, "that nine out of ten of those couples left my office together and I stayed poor." We all laughed!

"We didn't have much in those days," Harold said, again looking over at Evelyn, whose face reflected that she shared his values, "but we were rich in heart."

As the significance of this account was sinking in, I realized that this former law professor must have profoundly influenced many law students who practiced after him. "How many law professors are teaching these kinds of ethics today?" I asked Harold.

"Obviously, if you look at the modern lawyer, it can't be too many," he replied.

I believe that the ethics of many professionals, including lawyers, counselors, clergy and educators, do impact socio-logical change. For example, the attorney is in a position either to offer aid toward reconciliation, to accommodate the client's request or to exploit the situation for all the profit he or she can gain. Attorneys are well aware of the high profits that can be gained from heightening the tension between marriage partners—and some, not all, do it quite well.

One thing these types of professionals need to face up to is that people in crises, such as a marriage crisis, are indeed affected by the professional's ethics, opinions and biases. In the last quarter century, liberal thinking has advanced the idea that to have an open mind means never to judge anything. I heard one speaker illustrate this point by stating that most people today are like baby ostriches: "their eyes are still closed, but their mouths are wide open."

A popular philosophy is that "if it feels good, do it." The implied flip side to that philosophy is, "If it doesn't feel good, quit it." As a result, commitments often hang upon the feeble thread of emotional titillation and good feelings. The sad epilogue to this attitude in society is that it is taking its toll on the family and the children are paying a high price because of it—emotionally, psychologically, physically and spiritually. Children often lose spiritual hope because of bitterness and skepticism over any lasting relationship. This outlook results from experiencing too many broken ties.

There is no way to avoid this issue when talking about the self-destructive ethic. A teenager who is hurt is vulnerable to self-destructiveness. A teenager who is angry is vulnerable. A teenager who is hopeless and despondent is vulnerable. And a teenager who lives through a separation and divorce situation will experience hurt, anger and despondency.

A LOOK AT THE POSITIVE SIDE

A couple of years ago I was at the University of South Carolina attending a conference on the crisis in ethics and values in America. Experts were gathered from the educational, religious and human service sectors of society to discuss what must be done to reverse the downhill spiral of America's ethics. One message that stood out in my mind was delivered by Dr. Armand Mayo Nicoli, the head of the psychiatric department at Harvard. He opened his speech by stating that whether the audience wanted to admit it or not, most people know that many of the problems facing our society today are related to the breakdown of the family unit. "We have seen enough studies telling us what is wrong with the family unit. What we need now is for someone to demonstrate what is right with those families that are cohesive and successful."

Dr. Nicoli said that, over a period of time, researchers at Harvard University had studied families that had held together. They identified some common denominators of these families. The first was "commitment." These families had a strong commitment to the concept of commitment.

The second common denominator was "accessibility." The marriage partners were accessible both to one another and to their children. I noticed some people in the conference shifting nervously in their seats as Dr. Nicoli explained this point by saying in essence: "By accessibility, I do not mean physical accessibility. Many fathers say, 'I am here, aren't I?' Maybe, they're present while reading the newspaper or watching the television, but they are not being emotionally accessible to the members of the family."

His final point was that these cohesive families had a mutual, spiritual commitment. They worshiped together, they discussed their faith and they drew strength from it. In addition, they were better able to forgive one another when wrongs were incurred and, hence, were better able to deal with bitterness and anger—the major stimulus in separating family units. Upon hearing this I had to grin to myself. Unless I was mistaken, I had just heard a Harvard department head assert, from a scientific point of view, that the "family who prays together, stays together."

Pulling Together

In light of what is being communicated by society at large, it is increasingly important for families to draw together, to be open, to be realistic about problems, to think together and to discuss ideals, values and ethics.

We all know that many teenagers are reluctant to talk to parents—it just isn't "cool." Yet, in talking with hundreds of suicidal teenagers, I realized that they are living a paradox. Although it is chic for teenagers to act aloof toward parents, seemingly unaffected by their opinions, wishes and desires, their sense of worth and self-esteem hinges almost entirely upon this interaction. These teenagers have told me that all they want to know is that they are special and loved unconditionally for who they are and what they are. These teenagers desire their parent's affection, even if they outwardly appear to reject it.

Be Honest

Parents must not be afraid to admit that their child could have deep problems and could become potentially suicidal. They should bear in mind that they are not necessarily at fault just because a child has severe problems.

For example, my parents were wonderful parents and I knew they cared about me, despite our typical parent/teenager conflicts. They shared positive values about life with me. Yet, at one point unknown to them, I went through a period when I seriously contemplated suicide. I was experiencing a philosophical crisis in which I could not find a logical purpose for life based on what was happening around me.

Parents need to be realistic and admit that their children are as vulnerable as any to the ills and destructive influences present in today's adolescent culture. Parents would do well to reflect compassion rather than shock and anger when their children are affected and traumatized by the world around them. Parents would also do well to share their own struggles and vulnerability, which could lead into constructive dialogue about their personal faith and how God strengthened them. It may be helpful for parents to reflect on their own adolescent struggles and confusion in order to enlarge their capacity for empathy toward their teenager's struggles.

INVITATIONS TO SUICIDE

What About Music?
The nihilistic and narcissistic ethic, as well as the message of destruction, is available today in a multiplicity of packages. The message comes through in some music, books, games and other fads. Of course it is important not to categorically condemn the influence of music on a teenager. Not only is it ignorant to do so, but it is also unfair. Such an attitude will effectively slam the door on any type of communication with a teenager. For example, I have heard many individuals make blanket judgments that all rock and roll music is a stimulus for suicide. This is no different from parents 60 years ago judging the new "jazzy swing" sound as a stimulus for rebellion. Because I work with teenagers, I keep in touch with their "Top 40," and periodically review the MTV countdown. This helps me keep in touch with their language and talk intelligently with them about which messages are positive and which are negative.

In dealing with teenagers, I have learned that they will inevitably go North if you point South. In directing them, I prefer to glamorize South, rather than trying to force them to choose South. I then let the teenagers draw their own conclusions that South is the way to go. In presenting positive ethics for life I often quote artists the teenagers will recognize. For example, I may quote John Cougar-Mellencamp,[5] whose rhythmic song says you need to stand for something, or you'll fall for anything. Another artist, Billy Joel,[6] sang about quitting. His lyrics urge not to give up when you feel like quitting, because you'll catch your second wind—after all we're only human. By doing this I am directing a young person toward positive messages from their own culture and away from those messages that are negative and destructive—without condemning their culture as a whole.

It is important to understand that, over the past 20 years, the influence of music and lyrics in the lives of teenagers has escalated tremendously. Evidence of this can be seen by comparing two polls which asked teens who their heroes are. One poll was taken 25 years ago and the other in 1988. The top two vote-getters in the recent poll were Billy Idol and Prince, two rock musicians who unapologetically present themselves as lewd and exploitive—and make millions doing it. On the other hand, the poll from a quarter century ago named John F. Kennedy and Mickey Mantle as the teenagers' most admired heroes.

There is a current, radical trend in music that seems to be heading further and further from any sense of health and decency. It is a type of music that grew out of the "punk rock" and "heavy metal" music trends. It is known as "hard metal," "black metal" and "black edge" music. The themes of many of the songs are explicit in promoting promiscuity, drug use, rebellion, hatred, violence and self-destruction. They are the anthems of those who already have a "chip on their shoulder" and the recurring theme of rejection in their lives.

Going Beyond Symptoms

Too many adult critics are quick to accuse this music and these bands as the source of social and emotional problems among teenagers. By doing this they are only dealing with a symptom of the problem teenagers are experiencing rather than identifying and dealing with their real need. Adult condemnation of these musical gurus only reinforces a teenager's bond to them and does not solve anything. I believe that if someone were to approach that teenager and attempt to meet his or her emotional needs, the teenager would probably lose

---

Displaying a respect for a teenager's opinions and a sensitivity to his or her emotional needs will bring greater results than adamantly condemning their culture.

---

interest in negative messages expressed through music and other forms of media.

To record every lyric from every song written by contemporary musicians who condone suicide and self-destruction would be impractical. Instead, I suggest that parents listen to their children's recordings. Your child's music, especially the songs he or she focuses on, is a "window to the soul"—a means of insight into the state of his or her emotions. It is possible that the teenager may not be aware of all of the lyrics in the songs he or she listens to. Before asserting what you think of the lyrics, ask your teenager what he or she thinks; then, discuss their message.

I remember talking to one teenager whose father tactfully asked him what he thought of several songs, the messages they conveyed and how those messages fit into his personal philosophy of life. The teenager said that his father talked to him as an equal and showed respect for his opinion. Reflecting on his father's questions, the teenager realized that the messages in the music they had discussed did not correlate with his own values. As a result, the teenager quietly placed that recording at the bottom of his stack of music. Displaying a respect for a teenager's opinions and a sensitivity to his or her emotional needs will bring you greater results than adamantly condemning their culture.

I am not an advocate of burning or trashing a teenager's music. If teenagers themselves want to do so that is their business. If the parents dispose of the music, the teen will most likely go to a friend's house or to a car and listen to the music. Parents who do this will only widen the gap between themselves and their teenager.

Violence and Satanism

Another symptom of the self-destructive ethic in our society is violence. Violence has always been popular, but probably never as in vogue as it is today. From the time the Romans gathered in the Coliseum to watch Christians be devoured by lions, to today's hockey game, violence has provided society with an avenue to vent negative feelings. Today, violence has saturated society. Television programs are filled with displays of violence. By the time he or she is 18 years old, the average teenager will probably witness hundreds of thousands of acts of violence through television. Beginning with cartoons, violence continues through sports and semi-sports such as all-star wrestling and into television programs and movies.

What does this trend toward violence in media have to do with suicide? The more acceptable violence becomes, the more palatable and glamorous self-inflicted violence appears. This is reflected in the phenomenal popularity of games such as *Dungeons and Dragons* and increasing involvement in the occult and satanism. It is difficult for a person to ponder love, affection, gentleness and kindness when he is surrounded by pictures of violence. Instead, violence often leads to thoughts of hatred and the desire to see harm done to others. For many individuals the desire to see harm done is directed toward the person looking back at them in the mirror. Because of this, outlets that provide a forum, either in fantasy or reality, to ventilate those feelings are alluring.

The fantasy role-playing game *Dungeons and Dragons* has been linked conclusively to a number of teenage suicides and other acts of violence.[7] The game requires players to role-play fantasy personalities from a medieval fantasy world: warlocks, sorcerers, demigods, demons. Players are required to imitate forms of insanity, including suicidal mania, homicidal mania and schizophrenia.

Players of the game designate a "Dungeon Master" who has god-like control over the fantasy world. The Dungeon Master puts players in situations. For example, the Dungeon Master may decide that a "Fighter" player will fight a "Magic-user" player in a castle full of trap doors and serpents. The game may continue for days, weeks and even months. Detailed instructions outline how characters can be strengthened by magic, poison, battle experience or even insanity. According to the *Dungeons and Dragons Handbook*, "suicidal mania" is a form of insanity that:

> Causes the inflicted character to have overwhelming urges to destroy himself or herself with whatever means are presented...the more dangerous the situation or item, the more likely the individual is to act self-destructively.[8]

In 1982, Patricia Pulling's 16-year-old son killed himself after another *Dungeons and Dragons* player put a curse on him. To this day, Mrs. Pulling can recite the curse: "Your soul is mine. I choose the time. At my command, you leave the land.

A follower of evil, a killer of man." Her son's suicide note said, "I am being summoned to do this. I must rid the world of this evil."

Mrs. Pulling, of Richmond, Virginia, later founded a group called B.A.D.D.—"Bothered About *Dungeons and Dragons*." She claims that since 1973, when the game first became available, it has been linked with 120 suicides. Defenders of the game say that the connection is absurd, that it is only a game—simply make-believe.

One of the greatest threats in society today is the phenomenal rise in interest and involvement in the occult—specifically, satanism. Along with this rising interest in the occult is an alarming increase in occult-related crimes committed by teenagers.[9]

The Satanic doctrines are bold contradictions of Scripture. In satanism, hatred, exploitation, manipulation and self-indulgence are the rule, whereas Scripture promises and promotes peace of heart, contentment, love and eternal life. Those involved in satanism are clearly empty and desperately searching. They stand in dire need of what the Scriptures promise—but they are looking in the wrong place.

Until one learns to be directed by spirits, satanism is a self-styled, self-directed religion. The ultimate acts of worship for the serious satanist are homicide and/or suicide. Although the trend toward satanism seems to be in its embryonic stage at this point, stories of satanic suicides are appearing with alarming frequency.

These developments in adolescent culture, or what I refer to as "fatal fads," are symptomatic of an empty adolescent ethic and a misdirected ideology about the value of life. Before teens can be encouraged to live, they must discover why they should want to live. Questions about the purpose of life cannot be explained by pat answers because they are moral and spiritual in nature. We must restore a moral and spiritual climate conducive to finding answers as profound as the questions. Some guidance I can offer is that through Christ, I found that His purpose could become my purpose. So, I cannot define point by point a struggling young person's purpose in life, but I can point them to Someone who can.

Easy answers also escape us when we ask why this self-destructive trend is happening. After talking to thousands who have contemplated suicide, many of whom have attempted suicide and hundreds who have lost a loved one to suicide, the only explanation I can give is that it is happening because it is happening. In other words, the more socially acceptable suicide becomes and the more exposed people are to it on a personal level, the more momentum it gains. Suicide has become a self-propelling, self-destructive force. Like it or not, suicide has become a viable option for today's teenager in crisis.

Notes
1. Allan Bloom, *The Closing of the American Mind: Education and the Crisis of Reason* (New York: Simon & Schuster, Inc., 1987). As cited in *Reader's Digest*, October 1987.
2. Bloom, *The Closing of the American Mind: Education and the Crisis of Reason.* As cited in *Reader's Digest*, October 1987.
3. J. L. McIntosh, *U. S. Suicide: 1987 Official Final Data* (Hyattsville, MD: National Center for Health Statistics, 1987), p.1.
4. Dr. Steven Stack, *Youth Suicide: The Distressing Signs* (Pennsylvania: Pennsylvania State, July 1987).
5. John Cougar-Mellencamp, "You've got to stand for somethin'" from the album "Scarecrow" (Polygram Records, 1985).
6. Billy Joel, "You're only human" (Second Wind) from the album "Greatest Hits Volume 1 & 2" (CBS Records, 1985).
7. *Dungeons and Dragons: Only a Game?* pamphlet (Fort Worth, TX: Pro-Family Forum).
8. Ibid.
9. For more information about occult-related crime you may want to contact: Larry Jones, Cult Crime Network, Inc., 222 North Latah Street, Boise, Idaho 83706. Mr. Jones is an ex-law enforcement official who publishes a newsletter about occult-related crime in the United States.

THREE

A Generation in Pain
What Teens Are Saying Behind Closed Doors

SUICIDE is not so much the desire to die as it is the fear of living.

I had just spoken during a school assembly about those who might be suicidal and how to help them find reasons to keep on living. At the end of my talk I usually invite those who can "relate to what I am talking about today or know someone who needs help" to meet with me afterwards. It is interesting to watch them file into the room

I see the students look up and down the hall just before entering the room, trying to catch a glimpse of anyone who might see them come in. I ask the school administration to set aside a room that is as far from student traffic as possible. That way those who want to talk do not have to walk down a "corridor of curiosity" to get there.

During a session with about 20 junior high students, Brian was the first to speak. "All my brothers were star athletes—all-conference or all-state in basketball," Brian began, seemingly unafraid to talk. "What makes matters worse," Brian continued, "is that all my brothers—four of them—had 4.0 grade point averages. Not one of them ever came home with less than a 4.0 in all of junior high or high school."

Brian was a handsome, dark-haired 14-year-old, groomed in typical "preppy" fashion. As he continued to share, I sensed that he was a little uncomfortable with his appearance. It may be that part of Brian desired to look the way he did—wearing a crisp, buttoned-down shirt, a letter jacket awaiting pins, new deck shoes. But Brian also seemed to feel that his appearance was a false front—like he was trying to be like his brothers and was not performing to their standards. Or maybe Brian felt he needed to act superior—like a rich kid—rather than allowing his peers to see he was a normal person whose life was not as enviable as most of them probably thought. As he shared this he paused, choking back tears. Haltingly he continued, "I...am OK at basketball...nothing great, averaging about seven to eight points a game." Brian's head dropped, "I came home with my report card the other day and gave it to my dad who was sitting in his chair." Everyone in the group nodded, affirming that, yes, their dad also sits in a chair. "I had gotten a 3.0 grade point," Brian admitted.

"Geez!" I heard a kid named Harry mutter. The group laughed, knowing that Harry's ultimate dream was to break the 3.0 barrier!

But quickly, everyone's attention returned to Brian. His hands were folded across the crown of his head. He reminded me of a person being punished in a stock. In Brian's case, the punishment was self-inflicted. "My dad looked at my report card and said...and said...'You can do better than this!'...and he threw it back at me," Brian choked. Tears were streaming down Brian's cheeks. He was no longer pretending to be the superior rich kid he wasn't. Instead, he was just another hurting, vulnerable kid.

We all understood Brian's message. All he needed from his father was eye contact, a hand on the shoulder and a reassuring look that said, "That's OK, Brian. As long as you gave it your best, I'm proud of you. And I love you no matter how you might perform. You are special to me."

Instead, Brian's father chose to look away in disgust, throwing the report card at him. As a result, Brian was filled with shame. Everyone in that room felt Brian's pain. We understood the pressure he was experiencing. And we understood his feelings of not liking himself, not measuring up to the standards of others, feeling unappreciated and unloved. All of the things that should have given Brian a sense of worth could not boost his crushed self-image. Brian was in that room telling his story because he was thinking of killing himself.

Brian's scenario is not uncommon. I wonder how many adults reading this are reflecting upon their own adolescent years and the experiences that have influenced their sense of self-worth. I am sure that many of you can remember feelings of not being able to measure up. A recurring theme in my dialogues with teenagers is that they, too, want desperately to be appreciated and treated as special and unique.

I have discovered that a low sense of self-worth, or having a negative estimate of one's self is one of the major problems motivating teenagers to consider suicide. As we all know, the self-esteem of the adolescent is under constant attack. It seems that, for every positive stroke a teenager receives, he or she must absorb 10 to 20 negative strokes. Even among themselves, their conversation is characterized by "cut-downs" or who can top who with the most cutting remarks and observations.

I am convinced that suicide is the most extreme expression of low self-esteem, of the feeling "I don't like myself." The multi-faceted and diverse roots of this self-hate run deep and wide. They rest in the soils of home, school and peers. Each environment holds a unique opportunity to affect and nurture a positive or negative self-image.

Young people's negative opinion of themselves may be altered through the realization that someone thinks highly of them. Personally, I saw this change for myself when I came to the realization that God loved me for who I was and offered forgiveness through Christ for all my wrongs. This opened a new and healthy perspective for me and about me.

I act as a "sounding board" for teenagers—providing a non-threatening, pressure-free environment where they can share their feelings and where their self-worth can be boosted. My observations about the causes of low self-esteem and the desire to end life are based on what teenagers have shared with me in these situations. Through dialogue with these kids I have identified four dominant factors that characterize those who are contemplating suicide: (1) feelings of worthlessness; (2) rootlessness; (3) neglect and loneliness; (4) not feeling understood and appreciated.

Feelings of Worthlessness
During a small group session, one athletically built, handsome young man shared that he had tried to kill himself because he felt worthless. The rest of the group sat with mouths agape. They could not believe that he, an honor roll student, starting quarterback on the football team and one of the most popular guys in the school could feel worthless. I

could almost hear the other guys in the group thinking, "If he feels worthless, what chance in the world do I have?"

Certainly outside experiences affect our self-worth. Successes and accomplishments bolster our sense of pride and dignity, whereas failures, mistakes and rejections foster a sense of guilt, insecurity and inferiority. But I believe the largest contributing factor in a person's sense of self-worth is found in the home. Positive self-worth is affected largely by parental appreciation and affection, shared values and realistic parental expectations.

It is commonly agreed that a child needs to hear from his or her parents and teachers four words of praise for every word of correction to maintain a positive self-esteem. Furthermore, a child needs to hear from his peers 11 positive words for every negative word to continue feeling good about himself. Most teens are not receiving these strokes from adults at school or from their peers. If they do not receive this needed encouragement and affirmation at home, they will look elsewhere—they may even turn to a negative peer group just to find some measure of acceptance. After all, even a "bruised apple looks good in a barrel of worm-infested ones."

Most parents spend a minimal amount of time per day (probably about 2 1/2 minutes) talking to each of their children. Most of that time is usually focused on correction and instruction. Subsequently, most of parent/child communication is correction-based. Yet a child needs a large percentage of praise for every instance of correction he or she receives. With this in mind it is easy to understand why many teenagers do not feel like they are a valuable and special part of their families.

While observing the influence of parents and the home on a teenagers' self-esteem, I have compared two situations: (1) the teenager who is excelling socially, athletically and academically but does not feel appreciated, loved or accepted by a parent; (2) the teenager who lacks popularity, is mediocre in performance but lives in a haven of love and acceptance, receiving from parents constant affirmation of his worth. Although the latter may lack strong social skills and may appear to have reason for low self-worth, he is, in actuality, emotionally healthier than the former. Part of the reason for this may be that when "push comes to shove" with his self-image, a parent's positive influence dominates society's opinion.

Rootlessness

Those who have a strong sense of self-worth also seem to have a positive sense of family heritage. Members of this kind of family are exposed to a legacy of healthy values such as honesty, integrity, industry, togetherness, faith, patriotism and endurance. A child whose family does not express a sense of heritage and positive values will require much attention if he or she is to develop a positive identity and sense of self-worth. If this attention is not given, the young person may not acquire a sense of rootedness and belonging. He or she may then become a candidate for delinquency, under-achievement and, ultimately, self-destruction.

Another factor that contributes to a positive self-image is a sense of rootedness associated with place or home. In our upwardly mobile society, transition and change are a way of life for many. We are seeing the effects of this transient lifestyle on teenagers.

In almost every suicide rap session I facilitate at a high school is someone who has moved frequently—at least five times in seven years—or who's home environment changes often. These teenagers are afraid to make friends because of the pain they feel at separation. They have little understanding of family tradition or experience of predictability in their lives.

Predictability is recognized as an environmental factor that contributes to a child's emotional health. Without the stabilizing influence of predictability, the resulting frustration and confusion may lead to thoughts of death. Many who have been affected by the transient life-styles of their parents have remarked that they do not feel they are as important as their parents' careers. They feel their parents have not taken into account their emotional well-being when considering a move for the family.

Although most teenagers are reluctant to admit it, what they most desire is their parents' acceptance, approval and attention.

This feeling of rootlessness is not only caused by career moves, but also by family separation. Some children of single parents have watched a succession of boyfriends or girlfriends enter and exit their parents' lives. Often these people move in and out of their house further disrupting the child's sense of home and imposing upon their lives.

Stepparenting, which is at a historical high and growing rapidly, is also a highly problematic and traumatic situation for teenagers. My rap sessions are filled with teenage girls who are abused by their stepfathers, those who are treated unfairly by stepparents, those in constant conflict with a stepmother or father, as well as those who feel replaced and unloved by their original parent.

This disintegration of the family unit has magnified the teenager's already pronounced sense of rootlessness. Many are unable to establish roots through a family tree because they are part of a grafted step-family vine. It makes me wonder (tongue-in-cheek) if in 25 years everyone in a particular community will be step-related.

Neglect and Loneliness

Another by-product of the ambitious, young upwardly mobile professional family (YUPPIES) is that their children, known as the "latch-key generation," are often neglected. The "latch-key generation" refers to those kids who come home not to a parent but to a locked door and must turn the key themselves to enter their home.

This scenario has created a diversity of problems for contemporary teenagers. Where there is no parental presence and supervision, there is an absence of guidance, discipline and attention. While some families are forced into this scenario for the sake of economic survival, others force themselves into it for the sake of materialism. If these parents could hear the stories of heartache and neglect that I have heard, they might think differently about their financial pursuits.

Julie's experience illustrates this. "Julie, why do you feel like killing yourself," I asked.

"Because my dad doesn't care about me anymore," Julie replied.

"What do you mean he doesn't care about you anymore?" I queried.

"He is never home. He works two jobs. He doesn't need to. I liked it the other way."

"What did it used to be like?" I asked.

She began to sob, "He used to take me fishing." The others in the group fought back tears. "We used to go on long walks. I used to feel so special and so close to him. He hasn't done anything like that with me for over two years."

"Have you ever told him how you feel or asked him why he wants to make more money?" I inquired.

"Yes," Julie responded, "I have."

"And what was his reply?" I asked.

"He said he was doing it for me." Julie looked up at me and her expression seemed to say, "Isn't that ironic?" Mimicking her father Julie said, "I am doing it so that you can have a better life."

The irony of her father's response struck us all. Julie looked around the room and said quietly, "The funny thing about it all is that I might not be around here to enjoy it."

Following that session I wondered about many things. Although most teenagers are reluctant to admit it, what they most desire is their parents' acceptance, approval and attention. Here was a precious, innocent child who treasured the unique and intimate fellowship she had enjoyed with her father. But their relationship was being polluted by her father's conformity to the ideals of materialism. Julie told me that a simpler life-style would have suited her just fine. Why wasn't it good enough for her dad?

I felt that it was time to speak out against materialism, but whenever I brought up the topic at community and parent talks, it was as if my words were weighted with lead. Parents would look right through me. I felt as if I was treading upon "sacred soil" and broaching upon the "untouchable topic." Sadly, these parents will greatly influence their kids' life-styles—and their kids' children will be affected by it.

A final contributing factor to rootlessness in a teenager's life is loneliness. For many young people, the loneliness factor intensifies when they do not "fit" into any clique or group at school. Their personality or interests may not conform to those of any defined group. This experience often results in isolation.

Isolation seems to be a common high-risk denominator of many suicidal teenagers. A major issue in a teenager's day can be something as trivial as who will sit next to him or her in the cafeteria or in study hall. If a young person walks and sits alone throughout the day, his or her perception of self may be one of an outcast or a loser. That teenager may then reaffirm this perception, embracing behavior consistent with the "distorted" perception. By doing this, he or she further restricts his or her ability to form relationships. This vicious cycle perpetuates and magnifies the loneliness factor and eliminates a critical component of his or her personal support system. Special attention should be paid to these teenagers who have difficulty networking with their peers.

Feeling Misunderstood and Unappreciated

Feeling that they are misunderstood or unappreciated is another common emotion that suicidal teenagers share. I constantly hear statements like, "I just want to know that I matter...for what I can do, not for how I measure up to somebody else." As the story of Brian (mentioned earlier) illustrates, children need to know that they are accepted and appreciated solely for who they are. They also need to know that their performance is being measured against their own level of ability, rather than by someone else's.

Probably the most frequent complaint I hear is, "I am sick and tired of being compared to someone else." Whether they are compared to brother Bill or sister Susie, cousin Katie or neighbor Nancy, such evaluations quickly erode the self-images of teenagers.

It is obvious that each person in this world is unique—cast from an original mold. Technology supports this assertion, discovering that no two people have exactly the same fingerprints, pitch of voice, hair color, thoughts, etc. We are each an original act of creation. Because of our uniqueness, comparisons are unjust and serve to disintegrate whatever self-love we might possess.

For the teenager, to be appreciated one must be understood. Our suicide crisis hot line once received a call from a girl who told our counselor, "There is no way around it...I'm going to kill myself!"

The counselor asked, "What is wrong?"

Adolescence is a state of constant change that often frustrates attempts to gain a sense of self-respect and purpose. It is a constant struggle for a teenager to find a niche of acceptance.

She said, "I just want someone to understand...to understand what I'm feeling."

The counselor asked, "Why are you feeling so misunderstood?"

She explained slowly, "Well, I took some pills—actually, I took a lot of pills—because I wasn't dealing with some problems very well. My parents had to take me to the hospital and when I came home, they said they wanted to have a talk with me. I was hoping that this talk would help me. But all they said was, 'We want you to know that we are very disappointed in you. Now, go to your room and think about it for awhile.'"

The young girl then went to her room and called our suicide crisis number, desperately seeking a reason to live.

I wonder what it was that the troubled teenager's parents were thinking. Were they disappointed that their daughter could not deal with pain and frustration? Were they disappointed that she did not share her problems with them? Were they disappointed that the community might be talking about them? Or perhaps they were disappointed that their daughter's actions might reflect poorly upon their performance as parents.

Buried somewhere in the shadows of their disappointment was compassion and concern for their daughter. This loving compassion and understanding was what she needed to experience. But for some reason they did not, or could not, communicate it to her.

Many parents feel like they cannot relate to their teenagers. The "generation gap" theory has dissuaded many parents from even attempting to bridge the communication chasm between them. Sometimes, however, just a simple "I understand" is enough for a struggling and confused teenager. If you as parents do not understand, and truly cannot identify with your son's or daughter's feelings, then merely saying, "It's OK" will often suffice. Even if the teenager does not openly share his feelings, an occasional query shows that you are interested and that you want to understand. On the contrary, quick and superficial judgment demonstrates to your teenager that you do not care about them and that your understanding of them is weak and narrow.

We try to forget the errors in judgment and mistakes we made during adolescence. But these experiences will help us understand the teenagers in our lives. As we all know, it is not easy to be caught between childhood and adulthood. Adolescence is a state of constant change that often frustrates attempts to gain a sense of self-respect and purpose. It is a constant struggle for a teenager to find a niche of acceptance. Judgment, ridicule, harassment and rejection seem to attack on every hand. It is extremely important for the teenager's emotional well-being and survival that the home front be a haven where he or she can be understood and appreciated.

THE ABILITY TO COPE WITH PRESSURE, STRESS AND TRAUMA

Another major factor that influences teenagers to contemplate suicide is pressure. Not only are today's teenagers facing many of the same pressures preceding generations faced, but they are also facing a myriad of modern stresses. These include coping with eating disorders, pressure to use drugs, relaxed sexual values, sexually transmitted diseases, broken homes, occult influences, friends taking their own lives and the competitive realities of living in a high tech, supersonic-paced information age.

In addition, the choices and opportunities available to today's adolescent seem limitless. The female today has many more choices concerning her fate than she had 30 years ago. Along with the positive aspect of new opportunities comes the flip side—new stresses. A young woman now feels obligated and compelled to do something significant with her life and to be someone important. This obligation is compounded by the overwhelming choices that are available.

Many of today's teenagers are ill-equipped to deal with the historical traumas and pressures of life, much less the new ones this modern era has hurled at them. Past generations were perhaps better equipped to deal with day-to-day pressures and difficulties. They had the support of family unity, firm religious foundations, well-defined ethical standards and roles. Today's teenager, however, has a 50 percent chance of living in a disconnected home, and in many cases has little or no moral foundation, often lacks guidance and direction from adults and sees peers destroying themselves. These teenagers have no idea how to deal with life—and death.

When I talk to teenagers about dealing with problems, I use the term "positive problem management" rather than "coping skills." "Coping" implies that a person is just barely "making it." For example, when I ask young people, "How are you doing?" and they reply, "I'm alive!" I sense that they are "coping," or merely surviving. My response is to enlarge their perspective on "coping" to include managing problems. I say, "You cannot solve all your problems, but with the right help and right resources, you can manage any situation."

This may seem like nothing more than a shift in semantics, but it does broaden the definition of "coping" in a number of ways. First of all, it embraces the idea that external resources or ideas apart from our own can help us deal with difficulties. Secondly, it challenges the "Lone Ranger" syndrome. Many teenagers feel that their problems are their's alone and that they can deal with them by themselves. It is popular to say, "I don't need anybody." This assertion denotes independence and confidence. However, adolescents who are struggling in this way to establish a sense of independence may find themselves in need of other's support. When this need arises, they will be alienated from those who could lend support. In that moment of isolation, they will yearn for the companionship of a "Tonto" they may have abandoned back on the trail.

Perhaps one of the greatest stresses placed on teenagers is the pressure to succeed. For the underclassman, success may mean earning good grades and excelling in extracurricular activities. For seniors, success may mean having a specific, well-planned-out career goal—or, knowing exactly what they want to do with their lives. For many, the realization of career goals does not occur for 20 or 30 years. By that time, plans made during adolescence may no longer be suitable and the person may hate what he is doing. Depression and sometimes suicide is not uncommon among people in their 40s and 50s who feel they have wasted their lives and have never accomplished their dreams and desires. The source of this problem goes back to the pressure placed upon young people to make career decisions. Often this vital decision is made before a young person is psychologically and emotionally prepared to do so.

Experiencing Failure

This pressure to make a career decision—to know and plan for the future—is a major contributing factor to the number of suicides that occur on college campuses today. The suicide rate for college campuses and among college-age young people is at least 50 percent higher than the rate for high school campuses. This constant pressure to succeed comes from every sector of society and goes far beyond the realm of making career decisions. It has led to an epidemic inability to cope with failure.

The issue of failure blends two major motivators for suicide that are outlined in this chapter: lack of self-worth and the inability to cope with problems. Failure—more accurately defined as the inability to process failure correctly—heavily taxes one's self-worth. If this "failure syndrome" remains unchecked, it can drain any drive or determination for achievement from a young soul.

Failure, in my opinion, is the most common yet least agreeable of all human experiences. We loath to accept the fact that, aside from death, making mistakes is the only guarantee of the human experience. Besides our own mistakes and errors in judgment, life offers us a wide array of undeserved disappointments. Therefore, it is imperative that one be emotionally prepared to deal with failures and disappointments. The necessary preparation is not the sole responsibility of the individual. It must be spearheaded by the parent and accomplished in cooperation with the school, the church or synagogue and the work place.

In the past two years I have heard a number of stories from

my hometown about teenagers who took their own lives after making major mistakes. Two of these teenagers, who were popular, athletic high schoolers, committed suicide within two years of graduation. One was caught in the act of petty theft on the job. Rather than face the consequences and shame associated with his actions, he decided to execute his own judgment with a fatal shotgun wound to the head. The other teenager was involved in a minor accident while intoxicated. He, too, chose the same exit from life. On and on the stories go.

What can we say to a generation whose options in dealing with failure include intoxication, escapism and suicide? I believe it is necessary to lower society's expectations for success without compromising the virtues of excelling. First of all, this can be accomplished by realistically redefining success. Success is not being perfect; it is not always avoiding failure. If this was true, then God alone has experienced success.

When I speak at a student assembly, I often ask the students, "How many of you, like me, have ever failed or made a mistake?" Most will raise their hands. I will then ask, "How many of you have *never* made a mistake?" Without fail, a few genetically-engineered smart alecks will raise their hands (as I would have done in my high school years). I respond by saying, "Congratulations, you have just lied and joined the rest of us because lying is a mistake." Following that I ask, "How many of you would say that you are a real loser?" Very few raise their hands, but it is safe to assume that, inside, many believe they are losers.

Then I discuss champions who have suffered setbacks and defeats during their careers. I bring out the point that losing and failing are not the issue. The issue is how we respond to those losses and failures. For example, one person may gain determination from a failure while another person may become despondent. Speaking in the language of teenagers, I tell them, "You are not a failure because you fail anymore than you are a hamburger because you sit in McDonald's. Just because you experience failure does not make you a failure."

I believe that the most valuable degree anyone will ever receive is a diploma from the "University of Hard Knocks." Inherent in failure are all the necessary seeds of success. When I meet a teenager who is suicidal and depressed as a result of a "failure complex," I try to help that individual redefine failure and success. Failure and success are profoundly relative terms.

The relativity of failure and success is illustrated by a long history of "famous failures." For example, a boy who was thought to be retarded because he did not speak until he was four years old was Albert Einstein. A boy whose teachers told his parents that he was so stupid that he would never learn anything was Thomas Edison. This man failed close to 5,000 times to find an element that would work as a filament in an illuminatory object. A composer who was told by critics that his work was hopeless was Ludwig van Beethoven. A young man who was fired by his newspaper editor because he "didn't have any good ideas" was Walt Disney. One of my favorite biographies is about a man who had two business failures, eight election defeats, one known nervous breakdown and once said, "I am now the most miserable man living. To remain as I am is impossible. I must die or be better." The man was Abraham Lincoln. American history would have been different had he chosen the latter option.

Edison promoted one of the best theories about dealing with failure I have heard. Thomas Edison believed that life should be treated as an experiment. If the experiment fails, then change one of the elements. If it fails again, change another element. Continue the experiment until the right combination of elements and variables are discovered.

These successful people knew that the greatest "classroom" in life is experience. The objective of each experience and encounter in life should be to gain wisdom and knowledge. Instead of mentally tallying personal wins and losses, one should focus on those things that can only be learned through failure.

Virtues of Failure

I have observed at least three virtues of the "failure" experience.

1. As I have already mentioned, there is something to be learned from every experience. For example, the benefits of asking questions such as: What did I learn from this ordeal? What changes will I make? or What will I keep the same? can help balance the debt of disappointment. By learning from this experience, I can avoid paying a higher price for the same mistake in the future.
2. There are things that happen abruptly in this life in order to get our attention. We then have the option of changing direction. The same wind that closed the door before you opened another on its way in. When disappointments break painfully and unexpectedly into our lives, we have two positive options: either regroup and try again or start over by looking for new opportunities. With these two options in mind, the ending of a job, relationship or other disappointing experience is not due cause for the ending of a life. These painful experiences can be perceived either as failures or as new opportunities for growth and enhancement.
3. A real jolt can supply the incentive and determination to make something of life. One universal human frailty is

that most people expend only the energy necessary to "get by." However, when we realize that just "getting by" is not enough, we can begin to learn to strive for excellence. This "pursuit of excellence" is accompanied by positive stress that helps us meet our deadlines and objectives.

On the other hand, an attitude of perfectionism can be accompanied by the bitter feeling that nothing we do will ever be good enough. Perfectionism is unrealistic and ungratifying. The primary truth that the perfectionist must come to grips with is that he or she is human and therefore fallible.

The perfectionist often tries to prove something to his own sense of inferiority. This sense of inferiority or "failure syndrome" is reinforced when parents, teachers or coaches render quick and harsh punishment for mistakes. For example, an athlete who goes into a game knowing he will be benched immediately after a mistake will be motivated by fear. This athlete will respond either by avoiding risk and not fulfilling his potential or by resorting to perfectionism, becoming dissatisfied with his own performance—no matter how "good" it is. This applies to any child, student and performer who is controlled by someone else's unrealistic definition of success. When a performer is given room to make mistakes and then learn from them, he will be more willing to take risks and walk more confidently into life's "winds of adversity."

Adverse experiences come in several forms—many of which include experiencing failure. These experiences include:

1. significant loss;
2. relationship struggles;
3. living up to externally imposed standards.

Learning to manage problems in these areas is key to

finding purpose and meaning in life, rather than resorting to death.

God's example of holding a standard of perfection in one hand and offering grace and forgiveness for failure in the other hand would be wise for all of us to follow.

Significant Loss

Romeo and Juliet is the most famous of the romantic suicides. At a workshop, I remember one father who shared his grief over his daughter's suicide. He felt guilty because he had not picked up on his daughter's verbal indication that she was considering suicide. She had told him how much she loved the story of *Romeo and Juliet*—especially the ending. The man shared how his wife and he awoke one morning to find their daughter's charred body in the driveway.

An area where today's adolescent is alarmingly deficient is in "grief management." They receive countless opportunities to grieve, but have few resources for dealing with grief. The dark cloud of grief comes through the death of a family member or friend, through parental divorce or separation, or through the breakup of a romantic relationship. These scenarios have been tied to innumerable suicides. For example, it is not uncommon for a teenage girl who loses her boyfriend in a car accident to commit suicide one month later or on the anniversary of his death. Perhaps the most frequent situation is the young man who commits suicide after a breakup with his girlfriend.

When talking to teenagers contemplating suicide after a significant loss, I often find it helpful to share the steps of the grief process: shock, denial, anger, loneliness and acceptance. I also share how this process works and how to cooperate with it.

Both times I strongly contemplated suicide were while

grieving because of significant losses. I learned that one's perception during these times can be extremely distorted and confused. It is important that major life (or death) decisions not be made during times of intense grief.

As I stated earlier, suicide is not the problem. The problem for these teenagers is how to deal with their problems. We need to prepare and equip teenagers to deal with problems like significant loss. I do not believe it is pessimistic to predict that every teenager will experience death and separation in his or her life. Instead, it is realistic to prepare them for this experience (e.g. encourage prayers, inspirational reading, journaling, counseling and talking).

In addition, we must also teach teenagers that feelings are always changing—even those that seem to overwhelm us. At times, each one of us feels like giving up. One day we may feel wonderful and that life is great, and the next day our lives can seem hopeless. We must learn that changing feelings are perfectly normal. When we learn this we can "ride out" impulses of self-destruction and try to focus on more positive prospects. The key for the troubled person is to talk to someone about the way he or she feels—and through this process, come to grips with reality.

Relationship Struggles

Many a suicide note has contained the message, "You are going to pay for what you have done to me." Because of hurt and resentment toward others, many individuals have chosen to end their own existence. It is their desire, through their death, to administer a sentence of lifelong guilt upon the offender. When dealing with this type of individual, I often ask if an insensitive and inconsiderate person is worth throwing away their life. The implied message is one of dispensing blame for their own sense of worthlessness and failure of the relationship: "Because you could not love me, I could not love myself. Because you do not respect me, I do not respect myself. Because you will not bless my life, I will not live."

Again, at the risk of sounding repetitious, young people need to learn strategies for realistically dealing with relationship struggles. Offenses by others will come. We will be hurt and we will hurt others through neglect or by commission.

One young girl told me, "I'm going to kill myself...because I hate my ex-boyfriend!"

I simply replied, "On the contrary, you must love him."

"No," she hissed, "I hate him!"

I said, "You would have to love someone an awful lot to kill yourself because of him."

She sat and thought about it for awhile. "Well," she said rebelliously, "I'm not going to do it then, because I hate him!"

"If you have something to prove to him," I offered, "maybe you can prove it by your life instead of by your death. What are your dreams? What do you want to become? Let your anger motivate you to do it, until it is replaced by the motivation of your own pride and dignity. By doing so, you will prove that no matter how much he or any other human being tries to impede your progress in this world, you are going to make it."

The flip side of this relationship struggle is that of being the offender dealing with the guilt of hurting others. The rules for dealing with failure apply here as well as the principle of asking for and accepting forgiveness. Forgiveness is an issue that needs to be discussed and better understood. Modern books on stress management, written from both physiological and psychological perspectives, contain conclusive arguments and evidence concerning the damaging effects of bitterness and the absence of forgiveness in relationships. Unchecked, the refusal to forgive or accept forgiveness may lead to both physical and emotional damage as well as impaired interpersonal relationships—perhaps for the rest of a person's life.

I have observed as many teenagers who are suicidal because of guilt from the pains they have *caused* as teenagers who are suicidal because of the pains they have *endured*. Both scenarios result in low self-worth. In order to help a child develop positive self-worth, he must be taught to both accept and dispense forgiveness—especially in intimate relationships.

Externally Imposed Pressure

Sometimes children experience tremendous pressure due to unrealistic standards of performance placed on them by their parents. For example, some parents pressure their child to perform in an area of no interest or ability for that child. Parents may do this to either vicariously live out their own unfulfilled dreams and goals or to maintain a sterling reputation before the public. It is important to note that these pressures may be either explicitly stated by parents or implicitly perceived by teenagers.

In addition, teenagers often feel pressure from peers to "look good," to "fit in" or to "be bad." The pressure to look good (designer clothes, the right hairstyle) is a dominant subject of teenage conversation. The preoccupation with outward appearance, which is nurtured by the media, has driven thousands of teenage girls to anorexic or bulimic behavior and to an almost incurable dissatisfaction with themselves. The pressure to be bad or to fit in may result in compromising personal values and facing unwanted consequences. These consequences may include an unwanted pregnancy, a criminal conviction or a drug addiction.

As hard as they try, parents often feel helpless in their efforts to counteract this tidal wave of peer pressure that is swamping their teenagers. And many suicidal young people express frantic frustration about the pressures that are bombarding them: "It seems like I am living my life for everyone but me."

Sadly, these hurting teenagers do not feel good about themselves and often are not prepared to deal with the inherent issues of life. These teenagers make up a generation in pain— a generation that has chosen to anesthetize itself rather than face its problems, to escape rather than confront its hurt and, sometimes, to give up rather than hope for healing.

FOUR

Dare to Care

Pᴇᴏᴘʟᴇ don't care about what you know, but they do want to know that you care.

"Well...I'll tell you what I would say if I were talking to a suicidal person," stated my armchair psychologist acquaintance, as he munched away, the television buzzing in the background. "If somebody says to you, 'I'm going to kill myself,' you look them right in the eye..." he glared at me as if to accentuate his point, then continued, "and you say, 'Go ahead.'"

I waited for him to say, "Make my day." I thought to myself, *This is great, the general public's idea of helping a suicidal person is the Dirty Harry approach.*

Here I was listening to the quintessential couch potato guru—a man who had amassed a world of knowledge simply by punching his remote control. And he was laying upon me a capsule of his narrow knowledge.

Dr. Couch Potato lacked both of the necessary elements for helping a suicidal person: the knowledge of how to talk to that individual and the compassionate tone with which to speak. While both elements are essential, compassion is paramount simply because all of the knowledge in the world cannot substitute for sincere concern.

One young girl whose boyfriend took his life in her presence was sent to a professional for help. She described the session for me: "He sat there thumbing through books the whole time I was there. He would ask me questions and flip pages. He never looked me in the eye. I knew by the time he was done with his questions that his only goal was to place the proper 'label' on me."

This personal account strikingly demonstrates the scholarly approach to helping a desperate soul. I wonder if it was the professional's discomfort rather than indifference that this girl was sensing. In my workings with various disciplines of the helping sector, I have often noticed a great deal of fear and trepidation on the part of those dealing with a high-risk suicide candidate. Their discomfort could easily be mistaken for lack of compassion.

LEARNING TO SHOW COMPASSION

I believe most people do care, but many of these people are not fluent in expressing care. An ability to express empathy is necessary in order to effectively deal with someone who is hanging by a thread of desire to live, yet wanting to die. It takes extra courage to express care when one is sincerely afraid.

To complicate matters further, suicide is an avoided, taboo topic. Often professional counselors and psychiatrists have minimal education in this area. A friend of mine, who is a psychiatrist at a leading health facility in America, told me that only four hours of his training was dedicated to understanding suicide. If that is the case for a highly trained psychiatrist, then what is the situation of those who are encountering suicidal young people everyday: school counselors, probation officers or youth pastors.

Despite what we may or may not know, we *can* make a difference by caring about the issue of suicide among adolescents. The first step is to care enough to become involved. The second step is to become educated concerning the facts about suicide and to promote prevention education.

Many are surprised to learn that the majority of all successful suicide interventions are handled by nonprofessionals. While I do not advocate jumping out into uncharted waters without some preparation and coaching, I have observed that successful intervention work is best completed by those closest to the contemplator. With teenagers, this means getting peers involved in intervention. In another chapter, I will explain how this process can work (and is working). A percentage of cases, however, must be handled by professionals. Most school counselors and youth workers I know readily recognize when to refer an individual to a professional for therapy or, in extreme high-risk situations, to recommend hospitalization.

Early in my career I was naive about society's attitude toward helping suicidal people. It was startling to me to observe how pervasive both ignorance and apathy about suicide were. For example, during my first year of directing a suicide crisis center, I began gathering research about how to run a successful suicide crisis program. My inquiries led me to call one of the most reputable crisis centers in America. I asked to speak with the director of the organization. When I identified myself and what my job was, he wittily replied, "That is too bad. I feel for you."

I then began asking him questions about his center's programs and procedures. Eventually I raised the question of advertising. Because our organization had an aggressive philosophy of advertising available services, I was curious to see how other centers handled this aspect.

"We have produced some award winning advertisements," he responded.

"What was the message in the ads?" I asked.

"Basically they were for fund-raising," he replied.

Being a director of a nonprofit organization, I could certainly understand the need for such advertising.

I continued my interview by asking, "How many calls do you get a year?"

When he told me the number of calls they received annually, the number seemed relatively low for the county of 10 million people they were servicing. I queried further, "Do you have television ads that encourage the suicidal person to call?"

"Listen," he spoke sharply, "we don't need anymore *?!& callers!"

I was stunned! I was not talking to a sergeant at a police desk or an emergency room attendant. This was a director of one of America's leading suicide prevention centers. I politely thanked him for his time and quickly abbreviated the call. After hanging up the phone, I sat and reflected on the conversation. I reasoned that it is not always safe to assume that people care—even those well-embedded in the helping sector. While most people become involved because they care, many fall prey to the "burnout syndrome" because of the volume of incidents they handle. But I wondered, *If I was suicidal and my last living act—my last hope—was to call a suicide crisis center and I sensed that the person I was talking to was just doing their job, I wonder how much motivation that would give me to live.*

Genuineness or Gesture?

Just how far attitudes can roam from the compassionate track was illustrated vividly for me at a national convention on suicide. The keynote speaker at the convention was a psychiatrist who told the story of an intern who had treated a suicidal patient. Despite the treatment, the patient committed suicide. Distraught and angry, the intern expressed his feelings to the psychiatrist. In order to help the intern deal with his feelings, the psychiatrist suggested that the intern go to the graveyard and urinate on the patient's grave.

The people at the convention roared with laughter.

I was stupefied—not only by the psychiatrist's suggestion, but also by the widespread response. Thankfully, as I looked around the room, I saw by the chagrin on some faces that I was not alone.

Later, as a convention center director and I discussed this incident, it seemed clear that the most important issue for this particular psychiatrist and intern was exhibiting professional competency and credibility. The intern's anger seemed to be caused by the feeling that his reputation as a professional was tarnished because the patient had committed suicide. Sadness because a human being had ended her life appeared to be absent. True sadness and compassion could hardly exist alongside such a crude gesture.

It is not my intention to shine a negative light on all professionals who interact with suicidal individuals. Rather, I want to reveal the reality that, within our society, not everyone cares.

The Impact of Empathy

In past years our center has fielded several thousand calls from people living at the "very edge." I cannot count the number of times our counselors have heard people say, "It is just so nice to know that someone cares." While the callers are aware that they have never seen and do not know the person listening patiently on the other end of the line, they do sense their sincere concern. Callers are often aware that the person listening to them is volunteering his time because of a love and care for human life and a belief in the singular preciousness of each individual. These counselors want to do their part in the hope that they can encourage just one person to continue living.

I write and speak publicly about caring because it is too important an issue to take for granted. I need to be reminded daily that if compassion does not motivate my work, drudgery will quench it. People want to care. And people need to know that others care. Our young people need to be awakened to the dynamic effect of caring for the welfare of others.

Young people do not need role models like Billy Idol and Prince, whose definition of love is purely pelvic and whose ethics are exploitive of others for personal gain. Rather, they need role models who have made a difference in this world— not by what they have gained, but by what they have given away. I have great admiration for the way Jesus Christ role-modeled His teachings. He asked nothing of His followers that He had not already given Himself. He exhorted them, "Freely you have received, freely give" (Matt. 10:8). Mother Teresa is just one who is doing this sort of giving. She, like many others, is great at caring for others because she feels greatly cared for by God.

This is the challenge I am offering teenagers today. A young person can begin realizing his potential and enjoying true contentment by using his gifts, abilities and talents to help enrich the lives of others. Those who "dare to care" might be surprised by the impact they can make on others. Someone with no tomorrow in sight might be turned around by another's simple act of kindness.

Laurie is a good example of this. At the end of my talk at a high school, I invited those who needed to talk or knew of someone who needed help to join me for a rap session. Although it took much cajoling and coercion for Laurie to get her friend Tim to come to the rap session, he came—although somewhat defiantly and patronizingly.

Tim is the young man I mentioned in chapter 1 whose father had committed suicide with a shotgun five years earlier. Now Tim had a shotgun rigged with a string on a chair in his room. Tim had spent the last five years, aside from his time at school, in that room. His room had become a personally designed solitary confinement cell on death row.

In that session with about 30 teenagers, Tim was the last to talk. During the two hours while the other students talked, I occasionally glanced at Tim. He seemed detached from the whole situation. He didn't seem to hear anything but the echoes of his own grief. Tim was accustomed to being alone with his thoughts, but finally he began to talk.

He talked about his dad. Then, he talked about his gun on the chair and the three bullets reserved for that "day of release." I think Laurie was glad that, although his words were morbid, at least he was talking. She appeared to be a caring, concerned friend.

Tim continued, "My dad killing himself has made me want to kill myself. But what I believe makes me want to do it even more. I believe that when you die..." he paused.

By now the entire group was entranced by Tim's story. Before, Tim had been just a guy you see around the halls. How could they have known about all the pain he was experiencing? The looks on some faces seemed to say, "I guess I don't have it as bad as I thought I did."

Tim finished, "...you enter a great light and every question you ever had is answered."

We all knew what the next question was.

I asked, "By the great light, do you mean God?"

"No!" Tim almost hissed the word.

I knew this was too deep of a problem to deal with in a group setting. I asked Tim, "Could I talk to you after we dismiss?"

Tim shrugged his shoulders, faced his palms up, and curled his lips downward into a smirk as if to gesture, "Maybe, but what good is it going to do?"

After the group of teenagers left, Tim, Laurie, and I walked outside. I said to Tim, "I would like to give you something. I have written a little inspirational book called *Seven Reasons to Keep on Living*.[1] Although my father did not commit suicide, I do understand what it feels like not to want to live."

We walked to my car together. I had to hurriedly open my car door to grab my umbrella as rain began falling with some force. Laurie, Tim and I conversed under the umbrella.

"Tim, I'm going to be forward with you and ask you to do a couple of favors for me and for yourself. First, I want you to read this book. Secondly, I want you to give serious consideration to disassembling your 'death chair.'"

He shook his head nervously and said, "No, I can't do that. That's my only safety valve."

I looked at him quizzically, "Safety valve?"

"In case things don't work out," Tim explained.

"Well, Tim, I want you to know that I want you to live. You already know that Laurie wants you to live. And we all know that your mother wants you to live. And if your father had known what effect his suicide would have on you, I think he might have chosen to live."

I knew that if only he would disassemble the death chair he would make a giant leap toward life. Because I did not want to be pushy, I pleaded, "Well...at least read the book...." I let my words trail off so as to imply, "and you know what else you need to do."

That night I talked to parents in the same community. My

It is reasonable to conclude that for most individuals, at the time they took their own lives, they were not "themselves."

---

talk was followed by the customary "question and answer session." After the group was dismissed, three or four people came to ask personal questions regarding suicide and the ones they love. Soon the room was empty, except for myself and a woman who looked to be in her 40s. I remembered seeing her standing there in the corner of the room waiting patiently for the past 20 minutes or so. I also noticed that she was holding something in her hand.

"Can I help you?" I asked.

"I am Tim's mother," she began.

For some reason her statement did not register immediately. Then I remembered, "The Tim I talked to today?"

"Yes," she continued. "I want to thank you for talking to him. He actually talked to me today. He never talks to me. He just sits in his room." She had the look of a mother whose last ounce of energy was lost in anxiety for her son. She looked so tired. She went on, "Tim asked me to come here tonight and to give this to you." She handed me a piece of paper folded into eighths.

As I was about to open the paper, I noticed that she was waiting to see what the note said. "I hope you don't mind," she said, "but I am so worried. And I haven't the slightest clue as to what Tim is thinking."

"That's fine," I said. "After all, you are his mother."

I opened the note to find, not a note, but three bullets lying in the crease of the page.

I wonder if Laurie knew how important her reaching out that day to Tim was—I never got the chance to tell her.

KNOW THE FACTS

As my armchair psychologist acquaintance so well illustrated, society in general, has embraced some erroneous beliefs about suicide. The most common myth is that *people who talk about suicide do not take their lives.* Statistics reveal that out of every 10 people who commit suicide, eight talked with others about it. Because of the seriousness of this warning sign, it is not safe to assume that an individual is not serious about committing suicide.

Another misconception is that *the chances of suicide happening can be reduced by avoiding the subject.* Those who are experienced in suicide intervention have found that the frequency of suicide can be reduced by simply bringing the subject into the open rather than treating it as taboo. From my experiences, I have discovered that the majority of those who contemplate suicide seemed relieved to have the opportunity to bring their dark secret out in the open. Many respond by saying, "I feel like a great burden has been lifted off of me just because I've admitted that I've been thinking about it."

A common misunderstanding is that *all people who com-*

mit suicide are mentally ill. While those suffering from psychiatric disorders are certainly at high risk, the total number of suicides among the mentally ill only account for a fraction of those that take place each year. By legal definition, suicide is an act resulting from a "temporarily insane state" or committed by a person "not in his or her right mind." It is reasonable to conclude that for most individuals, at the time they took their own lives, they were not "themselves." It is possible to be extremely unhappy without being mentally ill. Although many individuals who have committed suicide are "clinically depressed," for many their depression is due to situational factors.

Another myth is that *there is a certain "type" of individual who commits suicide.* After a suicide, acquaintances often say that the individual just didn't seem like the type. The demographics for suicide seem to defy these stereotypes. Suicide affects people of all ages, races, religions and socioeconomic situations.

Another unfounded belief is that *suicide happens without warning.* Numerous studies reveal that most suicidal people drop clues regarding their suicidal intentions—yet these warnings often go unnoticed. The failure by loved ones to notice these warning signs does not indicate that they do not care. The fault lies in the fact that society at large does not recognize suicidal indicators. I have heard many survivors say, "I had no way of knowing this would happen. There just weren't any signals." Upon further discussion of the common danger signals, these survivors often acknowledge that two, three or sometimes more indicators were present.

At first glance, the following misconceptions seem contradictory. The first is that *once a person is suicidal, he or she is suicidal forever.* The second is that *suicide attempts are seldom repeated.* We find that most individuals are suicidal only for a limited period of time, ranging from a few hours to a couple of months. If these individuals can be nurtured and supported through the unstable contemplation period, they usually will survive.

On the other hand, the odds indicate that many of those who have attempted suicide will try again. Statistics reveal that out of those who attempt suicide this year, 12 percent[2] will try again and be successful within two years. However, 88 percent, if properly helped, can be diverted from this action and will never try again.

Another common myth is that *signs of improvement following a suicidal crisis mean that the risk of suicide is over*. A repeated suicide attempt often occurs within three months of the first signs of "improvement." During this time, an individual may regain the physical energy and mental drive to again act upon his or her morbid thoughts and feelings. Individuals who have been hospitalized often "play" at recovery in order to be released and settle the minds of those around them.

A subtle misconception is that *there is nothing you can do about suicide*. After speaking at a community meeting, I was approached by a man who identified himself as a medical doctor. The doctor sarcastically asked me, "Why are you doing what you are doing?"

I quickly replied, "Why? Isn't it obvious?"

He answered, "You ought to know that if somebody is going to kill himself there isn't anything you can do about it."

He may have been speaking from his experience. Granted, there are those who have set their minds upon self-destruction and are unreceptive to any gestures of help. But there is not enough evidence that this is a predominant situation to convince me to give up the fight. Although there are no available statistics indicating the actual number of suicides that have been prevented by the intervention of others, we do know there are many people alive today because of such intervention. It is easy to find individuals who have contemplated or attempted suicide who will testify of the persuasive and rescuing power of another's caring act of intervention.

I believe that this myth is rooted in the idea that *suicidal people are completely committed to dying*. This point was vividly illustrated during an encounter I had with a counselor from the psychiatric wing of a veteran's hospital. Upon introducing himself, he declared, "Mr. Anthony, I want you to know that I don't believe in suicide prevention."

Suicide appears to be more a fear of living and dealing with the problems of life than it is a desire to die....the victim feels no hope for the future.

Knowing that Vietnam veterans are society's highest risk group for suicide, I was a bit taken aback by his comment. I asked him to explain his position.

"Well," he said, "I attended a professional conference where this issue was hotly debated and the participants were strongly divided. The speaker was lecturing on the topic, 'The Case Against Suicide Prevention.' I believe that adults have the right to make their own choices about their own lives. I also don't believe that I have the right to interfere with that choice."

I asked him, "What is the essence of your interview with a suicidal patient?"

"Well...I ask him two questions. One, why are you going to do it? And, two, how are you going to do it." (It was of little comfort to me to realize that my tax dollars were paying this man's salary and supporting his point of view at the expense of Vietnam veterans, their families and friends.)

As we continued to talk, I could tell that he was burned out. The source of his fatigue seemed to come from continual encounters with those who were going to commit suicide despite any help given. Also, because he had concluded that all suicidal people were fully intent on dying, he had destroyed any motivation for helping and intervening.

Fortunately this counselor's point of view does not line up with the typical mind-set of those who are contemplating suicide. Most suicidal people are undecided about living or dying. They gamble with death, hoping others will save them. In most cases, the person who commits suicide is pleading to be saved—right up to the time of death. Those who attempt suicide rarely complain when they are rescued.

In many cases, the individual attempting suicide does not realize how badly he or she wants to live until after the attempt. For example, a 17-year-old boy shot himself in the chest, missing his heart by a fraction of an inch, and suffered only a collapsed lung. During his ambulance ride to the hospital, he was moaning, "I want to live...I want to live."

In another incident, a boy jumped out of a tenth story hospital window after being admitted to a psychiatric ward. He glanced off of a car then landed on the sidewalk and survived. When the boy recovered consciousness, a staff psychiatrist was at his bedside. The psychiatrist told him that they were concerned that he would make another attempt. The boy assured the doctor that there was no need for concern. He said he had changed his mind and had decided to live. When the doctor asked when this change had taken place, the boy replied, "Just as I left the ledge."

Suicide appears to be more a fear of living and dealing with the problems of life than it is a desire to die. A suicidal crisis most often occurs when the victim feels no hope for the future.

PROMOTING PREVENTION EDUCATION

In our society, the word "suicide" brings with it feelings of uneasiness, confusion and fear. Rather than finding ways to confront this topic, most choose to ignore it. But suicide is a reality that teens are facing and will continue to face in the years ahead.

Because of some negative, poorly administered programs that addressed the topic of suicide, many are afraid to support any education in this area. For example, a questionnaire about death was indiscriminately distributed to students in a number of schools. It asked questions such as: How often do you think of your own death? If you could choose the time of your own death, when would you die? and When do you believe that you will die? The most common answer received in response to this last question was "in youth." Not surprisingly, many parents expressed concern about feelings this type of questionnaire might arouse—especially given the volatile atmosphere in today's teenage culture.

I fully support the parents' concern in this matter. However, these questions could have a positive effect if asked in the right setting and by the right people. For example, if a trained counselor were to ask these questions in a family or small group setting where feelings could be discussed and dealt with, they could help facilitate healing.

Previously ineffective and even damaging attempts at suicide education have blocked the road to effective education. Such necessary education should teach teenagers about the warning signs exhibited by those contemplating suicide, and also how to respond if a friend informs them of their thoughts or plans to commit suicide. In my experience over the last seven years I have seen an overwhelmingly positive response by high school students to this kind of prevention education. It is heartwarming to see these teenagers bring help and hope to the lives of their despondent, suicidal friends.

How strongly has the stigma associated with suicide affected adults in the educational community? While many are responding aggressively by establishing prevention programs and student assistance programs, others choose to live in the "dark ages" and deny that these programs are needed in their schools and community.

One noted authority in the area of suicide education illustrated this confusion by first writing that every student *should* be made aware of suicide indicators. Later, however, he wrote that it has not been proven that talking about suicide does not *increase* the incidence of suicide. This contradiction has only confused educators and the community and made them afraid to implement prevention programs. After all, how can you educate students about suicide warning signs without talking about suicide?

One month after I gave a number of talks on suicide our organization contacted each high school in order to track the students' responses, including any recorded suicide attempts. Without exception, the schools' counselors informed us that the students' immediate response was to come to them for help—for themselves or for friends who were displaying suicidal warning signs. Our findings indicate that, by appropriately talking with kids about suicide, many who would not have received help can be reached.

In the future, education can serve as a catalyst for preventative action. This education must come through families, schools, churches and youth services. Just as alcoholism has become "destigmatized" by mass education, I believe that suicide can be dealt with in a manner devoid of panic and fear. Students must be made aware of the danger signals so they can identify and respond to friends that may be at risk. I have found that in every community beginning to fight and win the battle against self-destruction, there has been at least one individual—a counselor, principal, superintendent, youth worker, parent—who has stepped forward, fought for community support and helped educate teenagers about the impact they can make against suicide. This process is neither easy nor quick. It takes persistence, conviction and courage. It takes a person who is willing to "dare to care."

Notes
1. T. Mitchel Anthony, *Seven Reasons to Keep on Living* (Tulsa, OK: HIM Productions, 1985).
2. George Howe Colt, "Suicide in America," *Reader's Digest* (January 1984), p. 98.

FIVE

When the Disease Becomes Contagious

THAT morning I had decided to come early to the office. While I was unlocking the office door, the shrill sound of the telephone jolted me and I dropped a couple pieces of mail. On the fourth ring, I managed to grab the telephone.

"May I speak with Mr. Anthony, please?"

"Speaking," I replied.

His vaguely familiar voice came into focus as he identified himself as the principal of a school in a small Iowa town where I had spoken about a year and a half ago.

"Mitch, we have a problem," he said tensely. He seemed to struggle with how to present the problem. "Let me start with yesterday. Mike, a young man who was a senior and star basketball player shot and killed himself. Because this kid was so respected and revered by the younger students, the atmosphere in the school is frantic. Talk of a suicide pact has begun, possibly involving six or seven others. We've *got* to get to the bottom of this. But we really don't know what to do. What suggestions do you have?"

"Number one," I replied, "you need to establish communication with all your faculty members. There must be uniformity in what you present to the students. Number two, someone needs to sit down and talk individually with each student intimately involved with Mike."

I could sense the principal was grieving. The despair and sadness that result when young people end their lives go beyond the ability of words to express. The principal's grief was complicated further by the rumor that a "suicide pact" had been made. He was feeling a great deal of pressure to prevent further deaths, yet helpless to do anything about it. ("Suicide pact" is a fairly recent term that describes a very serious situation. The decade of the '80s was filled with headlines about small to medium-sized towns being shaken to the core by the "cluster suicide" phenomena.)

Upon the principal's request, I agreed to come to their school early the next morning and talk with eight of Mike's closest friends. These eight individuals were rumored to be part of this "pact." At that moment, I had no inkling of the education I was about to receive. I was about to encounter firsthand the turbulence, paranoia and confusion that a friend's suicide can affect in the lives of the survivors. At this time in my experience I had talked to thousands of students about suicide and positive ways to deal with their problems, but I had only read about suicide pacts.

After hanging up the phone, I made a few calls to change my next day's schedule and to ask a couple of friends for their prayers. I spent the remainder of that day pondering the situation I would face in the morning.

I thought about a town 90 miles from where I lived. It had been devastated by a half dozen suicides and a number of attempts. I had talked with a number of people in that community and they all seemed to wring their hands in despair and say, "Why our town? Why, of all places, is this happening to our normal, small midwestern town?" In their despair, these townspeople finally turned to the Menninger Clinic based in Topeka, Kansas, for consultation and help. (The findings and recommendations made by Menninger's consultants will be discussed later in this chapter.) The dynamics that precipitated the atmosphere of suicide clustering in this community exist potentially in any community. With this and other communities' experiences in mind, I prepared for the next day's challenge.

The grey skies and chilled air were especially noticeable the following morning while driving to Mike's school. The few people I saw on my way to the school were looking down as if pondering the events of the previous day. Everyone is shaken after a suicide in a small town. The first thing I noticed as I walked into the school was a chilling stillness—a stillness uncommon to the hallway environment. It seemed as if everyone was going somewhere, yet not really paying attention to what anyone else was doing.

I walked into the principal's office to work out the details of the day. As I had requested, he had set up a private room where I could talk with the eight students who appeared to be most severely affected and who might be part of a pact. The school administration wanted me to discover the details concerning a pact, assess who was at greatest risk and recommend how to deal with those individuals. My assignment was to be counselor, comforter, consultant and sleuth.

The principal warned me that not all of those appointed to talk to me wanted to chat. Mike's girlfriend was one of those most severely affected by his suicide. The principal revealed that Mike and his girlfriend supposedly had not been getting along. As was to be expected, she was overwhelmingly traumatized by the event and had refused the opportunity to talk with me.

Once the fear of dying dissipates, the predominant roadblock preventing anyone from taking his or her life has been effectively removed.

One by one I talked with each individual, asking only simple questions. I knew that the pressing issue for the school was, "Is there a pact, and if there is, who is in it and how do we deal with them." But I was more concerned about how each individual was processing what had happened and how much responsibility each one of them felt for Mike's death. If these questions were answered, I felt the pact issue would be resolved.

As I talked to each student individually, I said that I understood the shock and disbelief they were going through. I also communicated that I understood any apprehension he or she might have about talking right now. Lastly, I reassured each one that because of the emotional overload of the moment, it was very natural to be thinking about suicide.

Slowly and hesitantly each one opened up to me. Some shared more than others. I asked each individual to describe his or her relationship with Mike and to talk about times spent with him. I asked questions about what Mike was like and if they had noticed any clues or signals as to his intentions. One girl disclosed that Mike had talked about suicide so much around close friends that he had become "the boy who had cried wolf."

Mike's best friend, Tracy, disclosed that the first time he heard Mike talk about suicide was four years previous at the funeral of an eighth-grade classmate who had committed suicide. Another student revealed that Mike went "up and down" emotionally and was frequently distraught over romantic relationships. Another student talked somewhat philosophically about the paradox Mike felt in his own life. On the inside, Mike was not really happy, but on the surface he seemed to have everything going for him: popularity, respect, tremendous athletic ability.

Six out of the eight students taught me something startling about the aftereffects of a peer's suicide. Independent of each other, all six stated that they "no longer had a fear of dying." Each time I heard this statement, I paid close attention because this was no coincidence. It illustrated the fact that suicide has a profound "soul" effect on teens who are survivors. Once the fear of dying dissipates, the predominant roadblock preventing anyone from taking his or her own life has been effectively removed.

Having a close friend take his own life communicated to those six the reality of death. In addition, Mike's suicide communicated undeniably that a certain means (in this case, a handgun) can in fact kill you. While this is something we all "know," it is something we really do not "know" until it actually happens to a personal friend or family member. At this point, many teenagers begin to rationalize, "If I wanted to, I could use a gun, rope or pills and kill myself. I could actually make that happen!" Reinforcing this line of reasoning is the vivid illustration of a good friend lying in a casket, finally looking serene and at peace (thanks to the skill of a mortician).

Mike's suicide also communicated the strong influence of peer ethics. For example, a teenager who loses a friend to suicide may rationalize, "Sure it is wrong, but if he can do it, so can I." The irony of this situation is that, while these grieving teenagers are devastated by and angry with their deceased friend's act, they find themselves contemplating the very same act. This paradox personifies the inherent confusion that death by suicide brings to survivors.

When rapport with the students had been established, I looked each individual in the eye and asked, "Do you know of or are you a part of any suicide pact?"

Seven of the eight said that they didn't know of such a thing. The eighth person, Mike's best friend, Tracy, answered ambiguously, "No, but sort of...in a way."

I asked him to explain.

Tracy looked listless. He pressed his lips tightly together as if forcing himself to stay composed. Staring at the table, Tracy talked about a conversation he and Mike had two weeks before Mike's death: "Mike stayed overnight about two weeks ago. We were up real late and we got to talking about real deep stuff...you know...like you do late at night. The conversation eventually led to our shared frustration with life and the idea of ending our own lives. It was not like we made a pact, but we both sort of concluded that if things did not start changing for the better, this was probably the way we would go. We both acknowledged that the only thing holding us back was the fear of dying.

"The first thing Mike said to me yesterday when he came to school was, 'I lost the fear.' I didn't know if he really meant it. Mike joked around a lot...but then again, why would he say something like that...it's not a very funny joke. Anyway, I feel almost obliged to kill myself. It was like Mike was encouraged to kill himself because I consented to the idea. I don't know if he would have done it if I hadn't agreed that it was a real alternative."

Although there was no actual suicide pact, Mike and Tracy did have an agreement of sorts. It was an unspoken kind of agreement that made it too fatal to come right out and say, "OK, we are going to do it. This is when, this is where and this is how." However, their mutual admiration for the idea and discussion of it had effectively formed an emotional covenant between them—to the extent that Tracy now felt compelled to commit suicide to avoid betraying Mike.

As I shared in the first chapter, shortly before his death, Mike told Tracy, "I'll see you in hell, my friend." This statement carried with it the inference that Mike was expecting Tracy to follow him in death. Mike probably felt that he was the brave one—the catalyst for a plan he believed they both wanted. Little did Mike realize the prophetic irony of his last words. Whether or not Tracy committed suicide, his hell had begun the moment Mike pulled the trigger.

After finishing my interviews, I gave recommendations to the school administrators for each student with whom I had talked. Because I did not believe Tracy was in a proper emotional state to be able to ensure his own well-being, I recommended hospitalization until his emotions and psychological state could stabilize. For the others, the recommendations ranged from therapy to observation. In addition, I shared with the administration my opinion that the pact rumors were rooted exclusively in the "agreement" between Tracy and Mike.

The other students' thoughts of suicide were strictly natural responses to a friend's death and were not linked to any formal or informal agreement. I do not doubt, however, that had this situation not been attended to immediately and aggressively, it could have easily developed into a "cluster" tragedy.

IT COULD HAPPEN IN ANY TOWN

Other communities, however, have not been so fortunate. The whole nation took notice when four teenagers in Bergenfield, New Jersey, committed suicide together by asphyxiation. An autopsy revealed cocaine in the systems of all four teens. Consequently, many attributed their deaths to the influence of drug use. But later, information revealed that their deaths were more than impulsive acts committed while being "high."

There are underlying reasons why young people commit suicide, just as there are deep reasons behind a young person's use of cocaine. Pointing to drug use and suicide as the problem fails to address the larger issues hidden below the surface.

It was later discovered that the four Bergenfield teenagers had lost a friend to suicide approximately one year before their own self-inflicted deaths. At the time of this friend's death, none of the four teenagers received any treatment. Although many factors could have influenced this, we vividly see the potential consequences of not helping teenagers deal with their guilt and pain after a friend's suicide. This suicide pact, which first appeared to claim four lives, actually claimed many more. Because of the high-profile publicity this case received from the press, a rash of "copycat" suicides broke out across America in the weeks following the incident.

Most cluster suicides take their toll over a period of weeks and months. For example, the community of Clear Lake City, Texas mourned the suicide deaths of six teenagers within 10 weeks. This succession of deaths began when a 19-year-old high school dropout shot himself in the head. Shortly after, two of his friends, both high school dropouts as well, killed themselves. The suicide "chain" spread beyond this circle of friends when a 15-year-old girl shot herself. Three days later, a 16-year-old boy hung himself in his garage. Two days later, a 14-year-old boy asphyxiated himself in the family car in a garage sealed off with towels. In spite of the circumstantial evidence, some mental health specialists debated whether these deaths were part of an actual "chain" or merely coincidental. New York's affluent Westchester and Putnam counties were also shaken by a string of 12 deaths. Police authorities were puzzled because over half of the deaths were by hanging. One victim had told friends that he identified with a male character in the movie, *An Officer and a Gentleman*, who committed suicide by hanging. The year before the Westchester and Putnam incidents, the town of North Salem, New York, was shocked when a 17-year-old boy hung himself three weeks after his girlfriend hung herself.

Plano, Texas, is a flourishing yuppie community outside of Dallas that has grown in the last decade from a farming community of 30,000 to an upper middle-class city of 100,000. In 1983 one high school student from Plano asphyxiated himself after his best friend was killed in a drag race. A week later another boy was found dead. By the time another year was over, eight others had committed suicide. Cluster suicides were quickly gaining public attention and they caused mental health specialists to focus on the reasons why many teenagers are susceptible to "copycat" suicides.

One family counselor in Plano noted that community stress may have played a role in motivating the suicides it experienced. It had undergone such rapid growth that few people had time to put down roots. Because of the city's high divorce rates, single-parent homes, dual career families and affluence, the counselor asserted that the community was "fertile soil for this kind of event." While Plano, on the surface, represents the American dream of growth and upward mobility, Carol Steele, executive director of the Plano Crisis Center warned:

> The thing that scares me is that there is the opportunity for this phenomenon to occur anywhere in the U.S. where there are some of these factors.[1]

All these communities found that when one suicide occurs, other kids who are vulnerable rise to the surface.

Each community that experiences suicide clustering responds in different ways. For example, Bergenfield, New Jersey, focused its energy on educating the community by setting up crisis response programs, teams and support systems. In Clear Lake City, Texas, psychologists trained the high school faculty and students to alert teachers and counselors of suicide warning signs observed in others.

Residents of Plano, Texas, used $150,000 in community donations to start a hotline for those contemplating suicide. In addition, local churches organized programs to educate people about suicide, strengthen families and provide youth counseling services.

In one city (mentioned earlier in this chapter which, for the sake of anonymity, I will call "Anytown") where six students had taken their lives within a short period of time, a thorough school and community analysis was performed by a team headed by Dr. Kim Smith of the Menninger Clinic. Because Anytown is representative of many communities, the findings and recommendations made by the Menninger Clinic can help other communities develop strategies for dealing with suicide. As well, these findings may help others pinpoint elements in their communities that may create an atmosphere that precipitates suicide.

The first three suicides in Anytown caused a sudden,

noticeable increase in the suicide experience of teenagers in this community. Other age groups, however, did not seem to be affected. Surprisingly, the teenagers who committed suicide were not close friends, although they knew each other. No evidence of a common suicide pact existed. The teenagers were from different social groups and their deaths seemed to be precipitated by different causes. Still, suicidal behavior can be contagious and stimulate more self-destructive behavior.

As a general rule, the greater the number of suicides that occur within a certain period of time, the greater the probability that others will respond to personal crises in the same manner. While no scientific evidence has determined that the second or third deaths would have occurred even if there had been no previous, recent deaths, it is clear that suicide has a profound effect on others. Suicide begins to be recognized by frustrated, helpless-feeling people as a powerful solution to life's problems.

A questionnaire developed by Dr. Smith was given to all of Anytown's 9th through 12th grade students. The questionnaire included 45 questions relating to domestic factors, personality traits, coping mechanisms, alcohol/drug use, contemplation of suicide, as well as personality and behavioral changes that may have occurred during the last six months. Later analysis revealed that those students in Anytown with a tendency toward suicide appeared to come from two types of home environments.

Common Threads

The majority of those who had made suicide attempts came from homes where there were major disruptions and unhappiness. In these homes physical action was often the response to conflict and means of communicating displeasure among family members. The extent to which family members got drunk, abused one another, became sexually promiscuous or left during periods of stress seemed directly correlated to the extent to which suicidal behavior was exhibited by the youth in response to crisis.

On the other hand, the second group that indicated suicidal tendencies came from homes where there was strong encouragement to conform, to contain one's anger and to work hard for achievement. This less conspicuous group had made fewer attempts but more plans than the first group. The Menninger Clinic felt that this group was also at considerable risk of suicide.

The questionnaire also revealed that many students in both of these groups were experiencing a good deal of depression which they were trying to numb with alcohol. This kind of depression often results from low self-esteem. Low self-esteem is often a by-product of a chaotic family situation, as well as a lack of encouragement to develop into a content, constructive, healthy individual.

The Clinic's consultation with students and leaders in Anytown revealed further interesting information. For example, once a number of suicides had taken place, many students used suicide threats and attempts in an effort to gain influence and control over those around them. By their actions, these students stimulated anxiety about suicide and made healing in the community and their own lives difficult. This angry, manipulative behavior was perhaps the most destructive pattern observed in Anytown.

The Clinic's research also revealed that the high school's junior class had the reputation of being a bad or troubled class. Some of its members may have been trying to live up to that reputation by attempting suicide. In addition, the townspeople often used this class as a scapegoat for the negative things that were happening in the community. The members of the junior class not only contributed to the destructive suicide/anxiety pattern, but were victims of the label the community had put on them. They tended to mold their personalities around their perception of being mistreated, misunderstood and depressed individuals. The junior class, as a whole, may have been trying to live out a group "romantic tragedy."

Overall, Anytown was basically a healthy, growing community with much in common with its surrounding com-

---

Because of its role in establishing the moral fiber of a community, the Church can be a major influence against the development of a sense of pessimism and hopelessness about life.

---

munities. There seemed to be no readily identifiable trauma in the social or economic fabric of the town that might have contributed to the increase in youth suicide. Anytown was a community concerned about its young people and the stresses of modern life.

Just like all other cities and towns, Anytown had several specific variables that prompted its contagious suicide experience. As mentioned earlier, the first factor the Clinic noted was the presence of many chaotic, abusive and poorly managed home environments. Rather than coping with and managing their problems, these families often resorted to impulsive behavior, excessive use of alcohol and/or drugs and violent threats or actions.

A second characteristic of Anytown was the pressure on teenagers to be "good" young people. Many who seriously attempted suicide came from families that had high expectations. These families wanted their members to be commendable and conscientious members of their community. The children from these families often felt they could not live up to the high expectations placed on them by others. They also tended to have high expectations of others. To make matters worse, they often kept their feelings to themselves. Despite their hard work, they usually fell short of their own and other's requirements. Past research and my personal experience shows that this group of youth are at the highest risk.

The Menninger Clinic's analysis also stated that Anytown's teenage suicide crisis may have been influenced by the relative absence of lively, constructive leisure time alternatives. As we are all aware, young people need a place to gather in order to "see and be seen." If the main avenue for this involves the pressure to consume alcohol, the teens who desire both popularity among their peers and parental favor feel increased pressure.

In the Menninger questionnaire, those teens who threatened or attempted suicide revealed that they felt suicide was an acceptable and appropriate response to one's anger or to feelings of pressure by peers or adults. After the suicidal deaths of two popular students, suicidal threats became a popular and effective means of gaining attention and making others respond more sensitively. Sadly, as more parents, teachers and community leaders attempted to be sensitive to the subtle expressions of unhappiness by students, the more attention the students expected and the more they complained. Suicidal threats and behaviors became a way of ensuring that they got what they wanted. The teens spread rumors of suicide pacts and then dismissed and devalued the help that was offered.

Quietly hiding behind this high profile, attention-seeking group, was a small core of frustrated and depressed high-risk students. The more suicide was discussed as an acceptable way of dealing with life's difficulties the more the risk of suicide among these truly high-risk students increased.

RECOMMENDATIONS FOR PREVENTION

Since many communities can relate to the situations and factors responsible for the tragedies of Anytown, they all can benefit from the findings and recommendations of the Menninger Clinic. First, they recommended that the community shift its focus from suicide to working together to deal with the community's underlying problems. It was recommended that Anytown place considerable emphasis on improving the general health and vitality of the community. Students needed to be taught how to manage their problems, work together and affect the system in a positive manner by helping others.

The next recommendation was to facilitate a survivor's support group. Survivors of suicide talking to other survivors is an important and helpful method of dealing with the grief and healing process. The Clinic recommended that this group be well-publicized and strongly supported by the community.

They also recommended that the city council work with a council of students to identify issues of youth concern and initiate programs to address those specific concerns. It was important for the city to display a willingness to listen to and work with teenagers.

Other recommendations included setting up a crisis hotline, forming crisis response teams and training teachers, police and emergency personnel to recognize the risk levels of suicide and how to respond properly.

They also recommended that all schools choose and implement a brief curriculum on suicide. The purpose of the curriculum was to educate students about depression, the ambivalence felt by those considering suicidal action and the meaning of suicidal thoughts, as well as to provide some training on how to handle both their own and other's suicidal feelings. It was also suggested that the school give special attention to smoothing the integration process of transfer students. One solution was to form a program of "student befrienders" or "partners." The students in this befriending program could make a self-conscious effort to help new students gain more rapidly a firm social footing and healthy sense of belonging in the community.

The high school was also encouraged to provide credit for those students who performed supervised volunteer work within the community. The benefit of helping others in need is that it often helps a troubled person put his own problems into proper perspective. The leaders of the junior class were encouraged to take it upon themselves to help formulate plans to improve their image as a class.

It was also suggested that the churches take a more active role in three areas. First of all, the churches should hire enthusiastic, caring youth ministers and develop more aggressive youth programs. Because of its role in establishing the moral fiber of a community, the Church can be a major influence against the development of a sense of pessimism and hopelessness about life. Second, the clergy were encouraged to take steps to improve or maintain their counseling skills. Third, the churches and other community agencies should develop extended marriage and enrichment programs. This would address the well-known fact that unhappy, traumatic marriages among parents are a major problem for the families of suicidal youth.

Finally, the Clinic recommended that some type of peer resource program should be implemented (refer to the TOUCH program described in chapter 7). A peer resource program should train students to talk with other troubled kids, to refer troubled kids for help and to identify the warning signs that might suggest they are becoming overinvolved with a suicidal person.

Our organization, the National Suicide Help Center, provides information, consultation and guidelines relating to a number of the recommendations the Menninger Clinic made to the citizens of Anytown. The Center offers educational curriculum for students, teachers and other professionals, as well as programs to help schools develop an on-going suicide prevention system. These prevention programs include a peer response strategy, guidelines for beginning a survivors group, as well as information for survivors of suicide.

Based on the experiences of the communities I have described, the suicide-cluster phenomenon could take place just about anywhere. There is no guarantee that your community won't be the victim of a suicide cluster or a contagious attitude toward suicide. But if concerned citizens aggressively address the underlying issues I have mentioned and follow the recommendations of the Menninger Clinic, they can nurture an environment that will minimize the incidence of suicide in the adolescent community.

Note
1. "As 'Cluster Suicides' Take Toll of Teenagers," *U.S. News & World Report*, November 12, 1984, p. 50.

Six

Preventing a Crisis

IF you have ever known or been involved with anyone who has attempted or completed suicide, you must be wondering how you can dissuade a suicidal person from this drastic action. This chapter will address those questions.

If you are in a position where you might be able to help a troubled teenager, it is important that you understand the methods of risk assessment and intervention. If you are not a trained counselor, therapist or youth leader, don't worry; the concepts in this chapter are presented with the layman in mind. It is important to remember that more than 80 percent of suicidal individuals who do receive help are helped by nonprofessionals. It is helpful to bear in mind that intervention is not so much providing the needed help as it is transporting that individual to the help they need. Intervention is a process by which we caringly confront an individual with his or her destructive behavior and then propose a remedy.

It is common for those who need counseling to never receive it. Instead, they flounder through life or cling to anyone or anything within reach. The effects these people experience often lead to dissatisfaction with life, family and relationship problems, unresolved stress, addictions and even suicide.

What a troubled person really needs is help from someone who is concerned, caring and competent. The person best qualified to help an individual who is contemplating suicide is one who is willing to deal with him or her on a "holistic" level—working with spiritual problems as well as psychological and emotional problems.

Before approaching a young person who may be suicidal it is of primary importance that you have accurately assessed the risk level of the individual. To make an accurate assessment, you must take advantage of a variety of resources. For example, input from the parents alone would not provide a realistic evaluation. A parent may observe certain behaviors and warning signs but be oblivious of those exhibited by their teenager outside the home. If you have input from that teenager's teachers, friends and co-workers as well, you may assess that he or she is at higher risk than the parents' observations indicate.

Adolescents often lead double lives. A teenager may be one person at home and an altogether different person around friends. While a teenager may act highly irrational at home and display bizarre or upsetting behavior, he or she may maintain a stable profile among friends and in school. Rather than being an authentic suicide or crisis risk, this teenager could simply be manipulating his parents. Accurate assessment, therefore, demands careful and comprehensive evaluation of the young person's behavior at home, school, work, and with friends.

I am going to present several tools to aid you in assessing a particular teenager's risk level. The first tool is the Person In

---

If suicidal behavior is suspected, the counselor should not mince words but directly question the adolescent about his or her thoughts, intents and plans.

Need of Support (PINS) scale developed by Stephen E. Lansing, former counseling director of the National Suicide Help Center.[1] The second tool is a general assessment chart that measures observable risk factors in areas such as behavior, academics, peers, appearance, health, family and school attendance.

The problem with many suicide risk assessment scales is that they often lead to over-assessment and over-reaction. For example, I read the instructions for evaluating one assessment chart which stated, "Give one point for each of the following factors and if three to four factors are found, consider hospitalization." Four of the factors in the list included "white," "male," "adolescent" and "coming from a broken home." Approximately 25 percent of the high school population in America would need hospitalization according to this assessment's recommendations.[2] Such demographic details are not as relevant in risk assessment as an individual's current behavior and life situation.

The PINS risk assessment is designed to give a quick profile of anyone suspected of being a suicide risk. It takes into consideration the person's plans to commit suicide, the intensity of the method that has been chosen, the accessibility of that method and the support systems available to that person.

THE PINS SCALE

Plan

1. Vague or specific
   a. Can the person give you details or is he generally considering suicide?
   b. Consider the following elements of the plan: how, what, when, where and how much.

The more specific the plan, the greater the risk factor.

Intensity of Method

1. If a particular method is employed, how soon would death result?
2. How knowledgeable is the person regarding the effectiveness and use of this method?

The greater the intensity and knowledge concerning the chosen method, the higher the risk factor.

Nearness of Method

1. Does the person have the tools or resources close at hand to kill?
2. Does the person know where to obtain the tools necessary to end a life?

The more readily accessible the tools of harm, the higher the risk factor.

Support Systems

1. Does the person have any support systems? If so, how well developed are they?
2. How easily can the person reach helping resources if an attempt is made?

The further the person is from support the greater the degree of risk.

While not intended to replace a formal assessment or professional counseling, the PINS scale gives the crisis counselor a quick evaluation of the immediate situation. As you ask an individual questions like these, write down the points he or she presents. This will help a professional counselor make specific decisions as to what action must be taken. Bear in mind that people are not machines and are not absolutely predictable. Every individual who is talking of suicide must be taken seriously. This is especially true for those who are substance abusers, highly impulsive or mentally ill.

The following is a more intimate and extensive assessment tool. It takes into consideration details from six major facets of a teenager's life. If there is a high frequency of the listed behaviors in a number of areas, we can safely assume that the teenager in question has high risk potential. This does not mean that this person *is* thinking about or *will* commit suicide. It simply indicates that the *potential* exists.

The chart is completed by the counselor. He or she circles the numbers that represent the frequency of the behaviors listed that the teenager is exhibiting.

Frequency Key: 1, 2, 3 or more reported occurrences.

Behavior	Frequency		
Sleeping in class	1	2	3
Class clown	1	2	3
Destruction of property	1	2	3
Breaking up with boy/girlfriend	1	2	3
Lethargy	1	2	3
Obscene language/gestures	1	2	3
Reluctance to communicate	1	2	3
Defensive attitude	1	2	3
Withdrawn/reclusive	1	2	3
Crying	1	2	3
Impulsiveness	1	2	3
Depression	1	2	3
Mood swings	1	2	3
Sudden outbursts	1	2	3
Argumentative	1	2	3
Inconsistent	1	2	3
Delusions or hallucinations	1	2	3
Memory loss/disorientation	1	2	3
Paranoia (student feels picked on)	1	2	3
Other: _____	1	2	3

Academic	Frequency		
Grades failing markedly	1	2	3
Handwriting worsening	1	2	3
Lack of preparation for class (pencil, paper)	1	2	3
Work incomplete/missing	1	2	3
Academic failure	1	2	3
Extreme dissatisfaction with school	1	2	3
Irresponsible behavior	1	2	3
Not staying on task/always behind	1	2	3

Lack of motivation	1	2	3
Other: _____	1	2	3

Peers	**Frequency**		
Dropping of friends	1	2	3
Peer exclusion	1	2	3
Avoidance of peers	1	2	3
Other: _____	1	2	3

Attendance	**Frequency**		
Excessive absences	1	2	3
Asking to leave room often			
(nurse, counselor, rest room, other)	1	2	3
Truancy (all day)	1	2	3
Wandering in halls	1	2	3
Tardiness to class	1	2	3
Cutting classes	1	2	3
Leaving the room early	1	2	3
Other: _____	1	2	3

Appearance/Health	**Frequency**		
Undiagnosed health problems	1	2	3
Neglect of personal appearance	1	2	3
Weight loss/gain	1	2	3
Hyperactivity/nervousness	1	2	3
Suspected abuse of drugs/alcohol	1	2	3
Other: _____	1	2	3

Family	**Frequency**		
Suffered recent loss			
(moved, divorce, death)	1	2	3
Troubles in family			
(financial, emotional, health, separation	1	2	3

Other: _____   **1   2   3**

Over what period of time have you observed these behaviors?

ASSESSING A TEENAGER'S RISK

A potentially suicidal adolescent should be referred to someone trained in intervention and counseling. This qualified person will be responsible for determining the seriousness of the teenagers risk. In life-threatening situations, the adolescent and the one intervening must understand that confidentiality can no longer be kept.

When high risk is determined, a qualified counselor will conduct an interview with the adolescent. Following are points that a counselor will cover to complete a successful interview:

1. State the purpose of the meeting;
2. Share specific behavior(s) of concern with the teenager;
3. Allow the teenager an opportunity to share their feelings and observations;
4. Provide the teenager with feedback concerning his feelings and behavior and clarify information he has shared.

Some important interviewing tools that will increase the effectiveness of the interview are:

1. Provide a private, safe place in which to conduct the interview;
2. Project a calm and caring attitude;

3. Express feelings of hope and optimism;
4. Offer emotional support.

The interview with the teenager should accomplish the following:

1. Determine the duration of feelings of hopelessness;
2. Determine the persistence and strength of thoughts of killing self;
3. Determine whether any plans to commit suicide have been made, the details of the plan and whether any preparatory actions have been taken.

NOTE: If suicidal behavior is suspected, the counselor should not mince words but directly question the adolescent about his or her thoughts, intents and plans.

High-Risk Indicators

The following are some *high-risk indicators* whose presence either singly or in combination could represent high risk of suicide.

1. Giving away of personal possessions;
2. Discussion of and/or making suicide plans;
3. Discussion of and/or gathering of suicide methods;
4. Previous suicide attempts or threats;
5. Scratching, marking the body or other physical, self-destructive acts;
6. Preoccupation with death themes—spoken and written words/music and works of art;
7. Expression of hopelessness, helplessness and anger at self and the world;

8. Use of dark, heavy, slashing lines and/or unconnected bodies in personal art work and doodling;
9. Statements that family and friends would not miss them;
10. Recent loss through death;
11. Recent loss through suicide;
12. Sudden positive behavior change following a period of depression;
13. Depression and instability at the anniversary of a loss;
14. Inability to accept help coupled with any of the above indicators.

If high risk is determined, the following plan of action should be followed by the counselor:
1. Do not let the adolescent out of sight;
2. Immediately contact other adults involved in intervention (school principal, person who made the initial high-risk assessment) who in turn will arrange necessary help;
3. Notify the parent(s) immediately;
4. Only release the adolescent to a parent or someone who can provide help (a close relative, psychiatrist, clinic, etc.);
5. Follow up to be sure that help has been contacted.

Medium-Risk Indicators
The following are medium-risk indicators:
1. Explicit statements of intent to end it all;
2. No concrete, specific plan to commit suicide;
3. No chosen method by which to complete a suicide attempt;
4. Lack of any significant support from family, friends, a professional, etc.;

5. The individual has not exhibited any radical changes in behavior.

If medium risk is determined, the following plan of action should be followed by the counselor:

1. Do not let the adolescent out of sight;
2. Contact other adults involved in intervention;
3. Notify the parent (if the parent is a major contributing factor to the problem notify another helping person);
4. Provide parents with information about sources of help;
5. Follow up to be sure help has been contacted;
6. If contact for assistance has not been made, provide supportive help;
7. Provide assistance on a regular basis until adolescent has shown signs of stabilization.

Low-Risk Indicators
The following are *low-risk indicators*:

1. Vague feelings of hopelessness;
2. No suicidal plans;
3. No explicit written or verbal threats of suicide.

If it is determined that the situation is low risk, the following plan of action should be followed:

1. Provide supportive counseling and refer the adolescent to an outside source of help;
2. Follow up to see help has been contacted or if individual has progressed on their own.

Low-risk persons will benefit from supportive counseling and family, friend and teacher support. Encourage them to develop these relationships.

Ultimately, if one is exposed to teenagers long enough, he or she will eventually face a crisis with teens who are at medium or high risk. At this point, a working knowledge of how to diffuse and stabilize a crisis situation is essential.

THE ANATOMY OF A CRISIS

When one or more stressful events occur, the affected person moves from a state of equilibrium to a state of disequilibrium. In this state of disequilibrium, people feel a strong need to restore themselves to equilibrium. At this point, the person has reached a "crossroads of perception" in which a realistic or distorted perception of the event must be chosen.

While the individual's subjective point of view alone often leads to a distorted perception of an event, the input of someone outside of the stressful event may lead to a realistic perception. A person who gathers adequate support will be more able to develop adequate coping mechanisms. This support will help them come to a healthy resolution of the problem, equilibrium will be regained and a crisis avoided.

However, if the individuals at this crossroads of perception adopt a distorted perception of the event, they will not be able to find or take advantage of available support. These individuals will not develop healthy coping mechanisms and their problems will remain unresolved, the disequilibrium will remain and a crisis will occur.

Another way to understand crisis is to dissect the different stages of the "crisis cycle." Stages are stimulation, escalation, crisis, de-escalation or stabilization/post-crisis drain.

During the *stimulation phase* the individual has not lost

control, but something has happened to cause the person to become excited and active. This causes emotional and/or physical distress.

During the *escalation phase* the individual begins showing obvious signs of distress. In addition to increased muscle tension, there is a noticeable change in the person's customary behavior—talking louder or faster, fidgeting with hands, posturing, rocking, pacing, moving faster or slower, etc.

During the *crisis phase,* the person becomes disoriented

The different stages of the "crisis cycle" are stimulation, escalation, crisis, de-escalation or stabilization/post-crisis drain.

---

and out of control. At this point the individual can become very dangerous to him- or herself and to others.

During the *de-escalation phase,* the person begins to "come down," although he may still be very tense. At this point, a gradual decrease in the individual's nervous behavior begins, although signs of distress and unusual behavior will continue.

During the *stabilization phase,* the person returns to normal behavior. The emotional and/or physical distress is either under control or has been removed. The person may then experience "post-crisis drain" because of the emotional and/or physical intensity and duration of the crisis phase. The individual's behavior may drop way below the normal level or "baseline" before returning to normal.

Understanding a crisis does not *solve* a crisis situation. Someone has to caringly confront the situation. This is where most people become "gun-shy." A barrage of "what ifs" begin to blur a person's motive of concern, often to the point of distracting him from taking the first step.

Based on my experience counseling thousands of teens, I will say two things: (1) yes, it is scary *before* you start; and (2) it is not scary *after* you start. When listening to the traumatic stories of teenager after teenager, I often feel fear. The "what ifs" knock at the door of my mind. But I have learned that showing sincere interest in teenagers, gently reaching out to help their hurts and persisting until a direction or solution for their hurt has been found, always supersedes my fears.

It helps me to keep in mind the analogy that it takes 80 percent of the fuel to get the rocket off the ground and the other 20 percent to orbit the earth. For me, the impetus to expend the energy for the thrust of getting involved comes from knowing that if I do not, grim possibilities can take a foothold. I am grateful for those who gave their energies at the low points in my life. I know I personally can offer hope to no one; rather, I am but a conduit for the hope that God offers to each person. This thought keeps me from getting discouraged at the prospect of helping despondent individuals. With that in mind, I will share the "nuts and bolts" of intervention and counseling with the potentially suicidal person.

HEARING, HELPING AND CARING: WHAT YOU CAN DO

Prior to a crisis, you need to have some guidelines to help you deal with a suicidal person, as well as some knowledge of the referral base in your area. Since you do not know when a crisis will occur, the "prior to" is right now. In terms of connecting an individual with the proper professional resources, keep in mind that he probably will never get help unless you provide the means. Therefore, dare to care, because you can make the difference.

The following are guidelines to use when a person you

know reaches the crisis point. These steps are for crisis intervention and should not be viewed as a means of resolving problems. For the person exhibiting suicidal behavior, intervention is only the beginning. He still needs to find a positive solution for his problems. You should then refer the person to a qualified professional who will help him find a solution.

Step One: Build a Bridge Between Yourself and the Person

A. Be strong and supportive. Speak in a friendly but firm voice.

B. Strong, stable influences are essential in the life of a distressed person. Be that person. Guide and comfort the individual by saying things such as, "Listen to me, I can help."

C. As soon as possible, positively reinforce the person for having the good sense to get help by contacting you. Express hope because of his action of seeking help and request time with the person.

D. Be warm, friendly, supportive and nonjudgmental.

E. Express the three Cs: concern, competence and confidence.

   1. Share that you care and his problem is important to you.

   2. Provide emotional support, giving the person confidence in the fact that you know what you are doing.

   3. Take action that will show that you are able to help.

F. As soon as possible, get as much information about the person as you can.

Step Two: Open the Door and Listen

A. A person who is in a crisis situation needs someone to

listen to what he is saying. Use "door opening" statements to help the person start talking and then listen. Don't worry as much about finding out what the person is feeling as why he is experiencing a crisis.
B. Make every effort to understand the problems behind the person's statements.
   1. Work at identifying the person's primary problem.
   2. Don't dwell on the problems, just identify them at this point. Remember, the problem may not be real; it may be the person's *perception* of what is real.
C. Identify the event that precipitated the immediate crisis. If you are unsure, ask the person. Tune in to what the person is feeling right now.

Step Three: Evaluate the Reality

A. How serious is the person about ending his life? Does the individual plan on taking a specific action or is he just tossing an idea around in his mind?
B. Find out whether or not you are dealing with a true emergency by looking at the risk factors.
   1. Use the PINS scale or, if possible, a more structured instrument to assess the person's risk level.
   2. If necessary, refer the person to an appropriate health or help service.
   3. Do not swear secrecy to a suicidal person; it could cost the person his life.

Step Four: Assess the Intensity

A. At this time, how strong are the person's emotions?
B. Assess to see if the person is seriously suicidal or just intensely upset.
C. Examine the person's feelings before looking for more facts. Help the person explore his or her feelings by showing empathy in your statements.

1. Do not tell the person about someone who has it worse.
2. Do not say, "Everything will be all right," or cliches such as "Pull yourself together."

Step Five: Take the Person Seriously

A. Do not dismiss or undervalue what the person is saying. In some instances, the person may minimize his difficulties, but beneath an apparent calm he may be profoundly distressed.

B. Every complaint and feeling the person expresses at this point is important to him.

C. Use yourself as an example only to share a true situation and only if it relates to the person's experience. Don't go off on tangents such as, "When I've really been down and desperate..." or "I've thought of giving up too."

D. Normalize thoughts of suicide. For example, "It's common for people to feel helpless and hopeless to the point that they think about ending their lives. Because you feel this way doesn't mean you have to act on it."

E. Trust your suspicions that the person may be self-destructive.

Step Six: Ask the Right Questions

A. Do not be afraid to ask directly if the person has entertained thoughts of suicide.

1. Our research demonstrates that harm is rarely done by inquiring directly at the appropriate time about suicide.

2. Getting the issue on the table and beginning to deal with it can have therapeutic value in itself.

B. Initial questions you can ask are:

1. Have things seemed so bad lately that you've been thinking of harming yourself?
2. How would you harm yourself?
3. Do you have these means available?
4. What would you want to accomplish by harming yourself? Would your action accomplish what you want it to?
5. Have you ever attempted suicide?
6. Why have you chosen now to do this?
7. What has been keeping you alive so far?
8. What do you think the future holds in store for you?

C. Further questions may include:
1. If you really did end your life, who would you want to find you? (This may give you ideas concerning a relationship that is a precipitating factor of the person's contemplation of suicide: Would that person feel a sense of loss because of your death?)
2. Do you think the method you have chosen will really end your life? (This will give you an idea of the individual's existing knowledge in regard to the lethality of his chosen method.)
3. Have you ever felt this way before? What did you do then to feel better? (This tells you about the resources and strengths he or she used in the past.)
4. What are you doing in your life that you don't want to do? What would you really like to be doing? What are your dreams? (Get the person focused on hopes of the future and away from negatives of the past.)
5. What strengths, talents or skills do you possess that can help make your dreams come true? (If the individual says, "None," do some brainstorming to ana-

lyze the person's strengths and needs. The purpose is to bring out his positive traits. There is no such thing as a totally negative situation, but during a time of crisis the person has great difficulty seeing that.)

Step Seven: Assess and Mobilize Support Systems

A. Assess if the individual has any inner resources that may provide support in overcoming the crisis.
1. Does he have a strong spiritual/belief system?
2. Does he have healthy mechanisms for rationalization and intellectualization that can be strengthened and supported by an effective counselor?
3. Does he have creative abilities that can go beyond the things you see right now? (Brainstorming with the person can help stimulate this creative process.)

B. Determine who the person's significant other is (the most influential person in his life), if that individual can be located and whether that significant person will be helpful or hostile.

C. Ask the person about his support system (friends, family, etc.). Ask questions such as, "Who would you like to have with you right now?" or "It's important I have someone to contact for you, who would that be?"
1. State affirmatively that you need to know who these people are as part of the help process.
2. His or her responses to these questions will help you know where the person sees personal support systems in his or her own mind.
3. If necessary, help the person identify the resources he or she needs to begin improving his or her situation.

D. Are there any other individuals that the person knows who may be able to assist him or her in this time of crisis?

E. Ask the person what is keeping him alive (you may have already gained this information during Step Six). If the person can give you any positive reason, this will give you a silver lining—hope—to focus on. Always work toward focusing on the positive rather than the negative.

F. Share from your own experience the resources that have helped you during difficult times.

1. Only do this after you have helped the person identify where he is in dealing with the crisis. If you bring yourself in too soon, it may seem as though you lack concern and interest in him as a person.

2. Sharing from your own experience provides a positive role-model for the person in crisis—it shows the person how one can rise above a crisis and go on with life.

3. Never make up a situation that does not exist. The person you are counseling can usually spot this and, consequently, you will lose credibility.

Step Eight: Take Action

A. Do something specific and tangible. Give the person something to hang onto.

1. The more specific the action, the better the person in crisis will be able to rely on it for support.

2. The person needs to have the feeling that he has gained something valuable from having talked to you (valuable in his eyes, not just your own).

B. Focus on the most critical issue and use positive problem management techniques to prioritize problems and plan a course of action. (See chapter 8 for more information about problem management.)

C. Have the person agree with you to do something constructive to change his situation.

1. Ask what is the minimum that needs to be done for the person to feel that the scales are beginning to tip in a positive direction.
2. Help the person focus on the positive and affect a positive turn in their attitude.

D. If necessary, take charge and be firm, saying, in essence, "I will participate in your life but not in your death. Right now we will do this."

E. As much and *soon* as possible, take away the person's contact with his main method of committing suicide!

1. Tell (don't ask) the individual to get rid of the lethal device (pills, gun, etc.). The more out of reach the method, the more distant the actual commission of the act will be.
2. Most suicidal persons only have a primary suicide plan. If you eliminate the plan, the situation is often diffused to a point where help can be accepted.

Step Nine: Maintain the Focus

A. Simply because a person states that he is past the crisis does not mean it is true.

1. The person may feel some initial relief. However, if the problem has not been resolved, that relief may only be temporary.
2. Follow-up is crucial. Make sure it takes place.

B. If necessary, meet with the person within a few hours following this interview. Offer yourself as a concerned and caring listener until more formal, long-term help can be arranged.

Step Ten: Give a Supportive Handoff

A. Arrange "islands" of support to be positioned around the suicidal person.
   1. Involve as many positive, caring people—including professionals—as possible.
   2. Immediately provide the person with information regarding the support he or she has available.
B. In some cases, if the person is confused or excessively resistant to accepting help, you may need to set a specific appointment for him to meet with a professional. Follow up to make sure this appointment has been kept.
C. Always follow through to make sure ongoing help has reached the suicidal person.
D. Stay with the person as long as necessary, but no longer than is needed. Doing this will build positive mental health for both of you.

SUMMARY: DO'S AND DON'TS FOR THE COUNSELOR

Do's

1. Take away access to the method the person intends to use to harm himself.
2. Use a positive approach that directs the person's mind to the most positive options available.
3. Employ a calm and understanding tone of voice.
4. Ask questions in a nonthreatening, constructive manner.
5. Try to relieve the confusion and helplessness the person is experiencing.
6. Help establish understanding—for you and the person in crisis—about his situation by using total commu-

nication and positive problem management (see chapter 8 for more information).

7. Suggest that the person's family can be a source of strength and support. (If the person seems to become agitated or upset by that idea, drop it immediately and move onto another topic.)

Don'ts

1. Don't sound shocked or embarrassed by anything the person tells you.
2. Don't bring in the idea of how the person's suicide will hurt his family and friends until you are sure that suicide is not exactly what he wants to do in the first place.
3. Don't get in an argument with the person. You will never win this type of discussion and you may lose the person as well.
4. Don't feel you have to solve the person's problems by yourself or that you must have all the answers. Trust in God and the strength He gives both you and the suicidal person.
5. Don't give up. You can do it!

In matters of life and death, one cannot afford the luxury of being smug. It is wise practice to consult with another qualified individual on how this particular person should be dealt with. You can never be too sure about your insights concerning a person's suicide risk level. With these techniques of assessment and intervention as your foundation, the next step is to discuss ways to meet the needs of a distraught or suicidal teenager.

Notes

1. Based on the PINS scale by Stephen E. Lansing. © 1987 by National Suicide Help Center. Used by permission.
2. Stephen E. Lansing, *Suicide and Crisis Counseling* (Rochester, MN: National Suicide Help Center, 1987), p. 40.

SEVEN

I Get By with a Little Help from My Friends

THE lyrics of a popular song from the 1980s articulate the universal human need for friends. The words state that in good times and bad times friends will forever be on your side. That's what friends are for.

For a teenager, not having friends translates into not being popular or liked. Feeling unpopular or unliked often translates into feelings of being alone and having low self-worth. This in turn translates into feelings of worthlessness and insignificance. And all too often, feeling worthless and insignificant translates into suicide attempts.

If one agrees with this logic, one can safely conclude that a teenager's greatest need is that of true friendship—or in an isolated teenager's case, any hint of friendship at all. Many of today's troubled teenagers feel isolated because they have minimal communication with their parents as well as superficial relationships with their peers. When confronted with a real trauma, this individual may feel like there is no one to whom he or she can turn. On the other hand, a teenager who has healthy friendships and/or communication with parents does feel like he or she has someone to turn to. This is often their saving grace when they are faced with a crisis.

THE RAP SESSION

When I talk to the student body during a large assembly, I begin by using humor to put the audience at ease. It has always amazed me how much more people will open up if you help them laugh.

After I have established a rapport with the students, I tell my own story. I share my feelings and heartache over some of the severe traumas I faced in my own life: the drowning death of my best friend, a divorce in the family, the break-up of a romantic relationship and the torment of being ridiculed because of a bad eye. While I share these personal hurts, the silence in the audience is almost deafening—teenagers understand pain.

I then tell the students of the two times in my life that I felt life was not worth living and considered killing myself. I share how difficult it was for me to admit to myself that I needed help from others. I also share that I had to talk to someone about my problems and my feelings in order to work through them.

Following the assembly I invite those who are interested in talking further about suicide to a rap session. It is common to see a young person come to the session for the sole purpose of supporting someone about whom he or she is concerned. The young person may attend the rap session with a troubled friend, but often the concerned friend will come alone. Many school counselors and principals shake their heads in amazement that kids will open up on a deeply personal level to a virtual stranger. I personally think I have an advantage in coming into a school situation the way I do simply because I am not seen as a part of the establishment. The students do not feel threatened by me.

I begin a rap session by having each person in the group introduce him- or herself. Next, I lay the ground rules for the session: "Number one, what you hear a peer say in this room, you don't take out of this room. Number two, we do not laugh at, ridicule or belittle any personal or sensitive statement that anyone makes. And number three, if you break rules one and two, I'll kill you. Murder I can justify; suicide I am against" (this is said tongue in cheek, of course).

I then ask how many in the group could relate to my feeling as a teenager that life was not worth living (hands go up). I then ask those who have contemplated suicide how well thought out their plans are.

Finally, I discuss the real issue of why an individual may think about suicide in the first place. Keep in mind that it is crucial to focus the kids on how they are dealing with *life*, rather than on their contemplation of death.

A Case in Point
There have been situations, especially in larger schools, where I have received such an avalanche of response to my invitation to a rap session that I cannot possibly talk with all of the students at once.

Such was the case at a larger, midwestern school. After giving the invitation for those who needed to talk to meet in the library, the room quickly filled up with 30 students. It takes about two hours to give the members of a group this size the opportunity to express and work through some of their problems.

Immediately after the session, the principal rushed over to talk to me. He asked me if I would be willing to come back tomorrow and hold another rap session. He explained that while we were meeting, an angry mob of students had formed outside of his office wanting to get into the session. Because the room held a maximum of 30 people, they were not allowed to join in.

I returned the following day to hold rap sessions with those students that were not allowed to join the day before. The administration divided the students into three groups of about 10 to 12 students each.

The first was an odd group—one I will never forget. Of the 10 students there, only one had a serious plan to commit suicide. Angie became the immediate focus of my attention. I soon discovered that this young girl's intense struggle was of a spiritual nature.

When I asked her what had led her to think about killing herself, Angie answered, "Well...it started...probably about a year ago. I was having a lot of problems with my parents. We weren't getting along. I was having some disputes with friends at school and felt like some of them were using me. And my boyfriend Eddie, whom I like a lot, kept trying to get me involved in satanism. He kept telling me how in control he felt. He said satanism allows you to manipulate people and things and get back at people for the things they've done to you.

"Well, I felt a need for power; I felt like I had no say about what happened in my life. Satanism seemed like the way to get the control I wanted. So, I started going with him to seances and we would have our own rituals...and I could really feel something. It was spooky, but it was exciting. I liked the excitement.

"But I knew this was wrong and I didn't feel good about myself wanting to hurt others just because they had done the same to me. But at the same time I felt I had an edge on them because I knew something they didn't."

"So," I interrupted, "is this when you started thinking about dying?"

"No," she answered, "that is just the beginning of the story. That is where these people come in." She pointed to the rest of the group.

"What do you mean?" I asked, suddenly realizing that everyone else in the room was there for Angie. I knew this had to be a serious situation.

"Well...Linda here," Angie pointed to the girl on her right, "invited me to a weekend retreat thing. I really didn't want to go, but for some reason I did. It was some sort of a Christian youth thing. One night they had a speaker. After he was done speaking, he asked people in the group to come forward if they felt like they needed to dedicate their lives to God. I just sat there thinking, 'I probably need to, but there is no way I am going up there.'

"I can't explain this, but the next thing I remember was that I was up there and I was crying and something was happening inside of me. I felt that the evil presence was leaving me. And that is where I met all of these people. I felt really good about myself. I felt like I was doing the right thing for the right reasons."

"That doesn't sound like a bad story," I commented.

"It's not over," Angie replied. "My boyfriend just wouldn't leave the picture. It really shook him that I didn't want to be a part of satanism anymore. We were starting to grow apart. I think he thought that I thought I was better than him now.

But, that really wasn't it...I just didn't want to go back to satanism. But as time passed, I kept getting lonely for a boyfriend to be close to. And I felt like Eddie needed me."

"Tell me what his home life is like," I asked Angie.

"Bad, real bad," she responded. "His dad hates him and Eddie knows it. Eddie says that no one is going to hurt him anymore. Well, we started going out again and I stopped hang-

---

Teenagers almost exclusively turn to other teenagers for help. Because of this, teenagers are in the most strategic position to help their peers.

---

ing around with these Christian friends," indicating the group in the room.

I could not help but notice the magnetic interest and concern of Angie's friends. They were listening intently to every word Angie said. I could sense they were hoping she would be turned around through this talk. I know Angie felt it too. Their compassion seemed to weigh heavily upon her.

She began to cry. Through her tears, Angie finished her story, "I just...feel so...bad. I'm doing that stuff again...and drugs...and I just hate myself. And I feel...so bad for...for turning my back on God. I just want to...die. It is the only way I can stop feeling this bad."

"Maybe there is another way, Angie," I encouraged her. "How does it feel," I asked, "to know that so many people love you and care about the decisions you make?"

She just buried her head in her hands, shaking it back and forth, faintly saying, "I know...I know."

I turned it over to her friends at this point. I asked them, "What can you offer Angie to help her feel better about her life?"

First, they assured Angie that they would support her decision to quit practicing the things that were destroying her. Second, they suggested that Angie renew her commitment to Christ and keep company with others having the same commitment. This way they could help her withstand the temptation to go back into satanism. Then they all took hands, formed a circle, and said a prayer for Angie. Some of Angie's friends were crying with her, but they were tears of joy. Each friend gave Angie a hug and went back to his or her classes. I thought to myself, *That truly is what friends are for.*

WHO IS HELPING TEENAGERS?

Surveys I have conducted have provided some crucial insight into the current crises in adolescent America. Teenagers were asked, "If you were having serious problems, who would you talk to?" Not surprisingly, 85 to 90 percent of the teenagers surveyed responded that they would most likely talk to a friend, *not* to an adult. Anyone who works with teenagers on a daily basis is keenly aware that teenagers almost exclusively turn to other teenagers for help. Because of this, teenagers are in the most strategic position to help their peers.

If one looks at the helping sector in our society, which I refer to as the "Circle of Prevention" (see appendix), one can observe some inherent problems in this system. First of all, many communities lack a network between services and agencies. In addition, these groups are often uncooperative or competitive in attitude.

But this lack of cooperation is not the main problem. There is a lack of connection between the helping sector and teenagers. These services—whether educationally based, legally based, church, parent or hospital based—are all crucial and relevant, serving a specific community purpose. But they are adult in composition. In my experience, I have found that although these services include teenagers in their focus, saying, "If you are having problems, come to us," the reality is that only 10 to 15 percent of teenagers actually will come to adults for help.

I surveyed scores of community leaders in these various agencies and services. I said, "Let's assume the figures are correct and 10 out of 100 teenagers will turn to an adult for help. Out of those 10, how many do you suppose get the comfort, encouragement and guidance they need?"

Across the board, the answer was around three. Although this represents a small number of those teenagers needing help, the circle of prevention appears to be quite busy. Whether or not this is the fault of the circle of prevention, the fact stands that few teenagers are getting the help they need.

Furthermore, if 90 out of 100 troubled teenagers are turning to their friends for help, it is safe to estimate that at least half of them are getting the understanding, encouragement and support they need. But this still means that approximately half of troubled teenagers are not having their emotional, psychological and spiritual needs met. Add to this group those teenagers who turn to adults for help and are not receiving the help they need, we have over 50 out of 100 teenagers that are not having their needs met. Although we cannot possibly meet the needs of all the troubled teenagers, there is much more that we can do.

Peer Counseling
Rapidly gaining prominence is the philosophy that if we really want to reach teenagers, we have to work through teenagers. We have seen the establishment of peer-helping and student-assistance programs in schools. These programs are student-based and focus on personal growth and crisis pre-

vention. No two programs are exactly alike. There are great differences as to how students become part of a program, how they are trained and what the program's focus is.

In recent years, the popular "Just Say No" approach to the problem of drugs and alcohol has tried to use positive peer pressure to establish a healthier ethic. Another example of this approach in prevention is the campaign against drunk driving started by the group Mothers Against Drunk Driving (MADD). This cause soon spawned another group, Students Against Drunk Driving (SADD).

Naturally, some teenagers are going to be for anything mothers are against. But a teenager might listen to a peer who is sharing the same message. Bear in mind that this is not meant to minimize the profound and pervasive impact of the MADD cause. The MADD group is responsible for getting the ball rolling and educating students on the lethal realities of drinking and driving. In addition, MADD is also responsible for providing alternatives to getting drunk at major high school events. However, there is no question that the SADD approach is reaching many teenagers that MADD is unable to reach.

Peer-Based Prevention Programs
Each school should have some sort of peer-based prevention program. However, I think it is short-sighted to focus these programs on specific issues such as drugs and alcohol, eating disorders or suicide. These issues are symptomatic of deeper, *internal* struggles. Lobbying a teenager to stop using drugs and alcohol does not necessarily resolve the problem that led him or her to use these substances. If a teenager is not trained to manage problems, he will probably return to drugs, alcohol or some other vice.

One problem that many school prevention programs have is that they, like many adult-based programs, operate under the assumption that if a teenager needs help, he or she will ask for it. This kind of program is what I refer to as a "passive helper." It makes no more sense for a teenager to assume that another teenager will come to him for help than it does for an adult to assume the same.

A major pitfall for many student-based crisis prevention programs is their high-profile approach. For example, the administration lines up the helpers and tells the student body, "If you need help you should come to these students." The philosophy behind this approach is that by recognizing these helpers, more students will be inclined to go to them for help. This is not always a safe assumption because often just the opposite occurs.

By recognizing a specific group of students and saying, "Come to them," we may unintentionally alienate them from the student body. For example, I once received a call from a principal who said, "We started a student-assistance program, trained a select group of students, recognized them before the student body and told those who needed help to come to them." Guess what happened? You've got it! The student body ignored and alienated those in the student-assistance group for the rest of the year.

Another danger in this high-profile approach is the way in which students are selected to participate as helpers. A natural inclination would be to select the top, most responsible and highest achieving students. These students are excellent choices if your only objective is to reach the top, most responsible, highest achieving students.

Another way student participants are gathered is through a voluntary sign-up. This process will identify some appropriate individuals, but it also will attract some inappropriate individuals.

If your purpose is to effectively reach as much of the student body as possible, it is imperative that you have a *healthy cross-representation* of that student body in a student-based helping program. These participants should represent the various cliques, classes and groups within a school.

Although students differ from one region of the country to another and from an urban to a rural environment, each school has many similar kinds of groups within its student body. Students are often classified by their interests, appearance, socioeconomic standing, intelligence and abilities. Teenagers give these groups labels such as "jocks," "motor heads," "pot-heads," "goody-two-shoes," "heavy metal heads," "computer heads," "dead heads," etc. If an individual does not have an identity with any particular group, he or she is often placed in the group known as the "loners."

A reality on junior high and high school campuses is that members of one identifiable clique have little respect for members of another clique. Because of this, parading top-level students in front of the student body and saying, "Come to them if you have trouble," is often perceived as, "These people are better than you. Therefore, you need their help." The unspoken response is often, "Not on my dying breath!"

These obstacles are what led me to get involved in a concept called Teens in TOUCH (Teens Offering Understanding, Caring and Help). This approach can work on its own as a base program or alongside an existing program. Following is a description of how the TOUCH concept works.

TEENS IN TOUCH

The philosophy of TOUCH can be summarized best by two catch words: *low-profile* and *aggressive*. I feel it is important for any intervention program to keep a low profile in order to prevent those involved from becoming alienated and, as a

result, ineffective. A low-profile approach also demonstrates
for those teenagers involved that sincere caring and effort are
more important than the possible recognition received for
their efforts. This keeps the students' focus where it belongs:
On the individual who is hurting, depressed and lonely.

If a low-profile approach is maintained, some may ask,
"How will anyone know where to get help?" This leads to the

**When an individual becomes part of a team, the group
works *together* to sort out and work through these problem
situations. Because the burden is now shared, the pressure
on the individual student is minimized.**

second philosophy of the TOUCH program. An effective intervention team will be taught to be *aggressive* rather than *passive*
in responding to forming crises. Rather than passively waiting
for troubled persons to ask for help, intervention should take
place as soon as verbal, behavioral and situational warning
signs are noticed by helpers in the program. TOUCH team
members are taught that if the problems behind the warning
signs are dealt with in their formative stages, there will be
fewer high-risk, emergency crises with which to deal.

A common objection adults make to the idea of training
teens is, "It sounds like you are trying to turn these kids into
therapists." Rather than being trained as "mini-therapists,"
these teenagers are being trained simply as bridge-builders
between the hurting person and the helping person. These
teenagers are taught the skills of vigilant observation and time-
ly response. However, they are also taught *not* to respond on
their own but through group effort and with program approval.

Another criticism adults have of student-based intervention programs is that it puts too much pressure on these kids to help others. Our experience has shown just the opposite to be true. Individuals involved in these programs already fit a "mother hen" or "watchman" personality profile. Their friends have been telling them their problems for a long time, but most of the time they carry their friends' burdens alone. This can bring extreme pressure on an individual. However, when an individual becomes part of a team, the group works *together* to sort out and work through these problem situations. Because the burden is now shared, the pressure on the individual student is minimized.

Three aspects crucial to the success of any student-based intervention program are: the process by which student participants are selected, the way in which these students are trained and how the program is applied.

Selecting Participants

We all recognize that no helping program is any better than the quality of the persons involved. This makes the process of selecting students to be involved in a student-based prevention program extremely important. If the wrong students are selected, the group may lose its focus, cliques may begin to surface within the intervention group and the ability to intervene may be lost. As a result, the school administration may become disillusioned with such approaches.

No single selection process can meet the needs of every school. Each selection process has certain strengths as well as pitfalls. For example, if participants for the program are chosen exclusively by the students, the selection process can turn into a popularity contest—especially in smaller schools. If, however, only faculty members choose the participants, it is probable that the faculty members' prejudices will enter the picture. This often causes certain groups of students to be excluded from the helping process. If a student sign-up is the only means of selecting participants, certain students who are not qualified may be chosen.

The TOUCH concept advises a combination of these processes. Students' suggestions can be helpful in getting the perspective of the student body. We suggest using the following questions to identify students' choices:

1. If you were having serious problems, what three friends or peers would you most likely talk to;
2. If you really needed to talk to someone about a problem, what two faculty members would you feel most *comfortable* talking with.

These questions can help identify the empathetic crowd among both students and faculty. Bear in mind that this process may upset some political applecarts if a janitor gets more votes than a counselor. It is not as important who kids are *supposed* to turn to as it is to whom kids are *comfortable* turning.

The group the students have identified can then be used as a base for selecting participants for a student-based prevention program. Once a sampling has been selected, a core of faculty members should screen the chosen individuals. Experience has demonstrated that a combination of student input and faculty screening results in a balanced selection.

Training Participants
A second important characteristic of a successful student-based intervention program is adequate training of participants. The TOUCH concept promotes the idea that training in the areas of caring and helping should be the program's primary focus. This concept also implies that this training should be an ongoing process.

Initial training should help participants:
- Develop communication skills;
- Promote an ethic of caring;
- Build trust between intervention team members;
- Work together as a team;
- Identify warning signs displayed by destructive personalities;
- Recognize the beginning of a crisis;
- Listen, understand and respond to troubled peers;
- Provide a troubled peer with the right help on time;
- Learn to confront without conflict.

Ongoing training helps participants:
- Build peer's self-esteem;
- Develop problem management skills;
- Supply participants with information about specific issues such as drug abuse, eating disorders, suicide.

Although many programs offer extensive training, they often fall short in practical application. Application is crucial for an intervention program to be successful. Scores of schools have gone to extreme lengths and cost to train students and then "send them out into the hallways" hoping they will come to the staff if they see anything.

I find it dangerous to presume that any single teenager possesses enough wisdom and maturity to differentiate what response is called for in any given situation. But if this teenager becomes part of a team of students and advisors that meets regularly, shares concerns about specific situations and discusses proper responses, the responsibility for responding to a given situation is not placed on individual teenagers.

The most important part of the TOUCH concept is that all the training in the world becomes useless if it is not applied through a formal caring process. Intervention teams are encouraged to meet on a biweekly basis. A formal agenda is followed in each meeting.

The first point on the agenda is *shared concern*. Each team member is given the opportunity to share any concerns he may have about possible crises he feels may be forming.

When all concerns have been aired, the students and advisors have what we call a *brainstorming session*. Team members explore all the possible avenues for encouraging and helping the troubled individuals they have identified. Then the group formulates a specific *strategy* to meet these individuals' needs.

Once a strategy is settled upon by the group, they move on to the *action plan*. During this phase individuals take responsibility for executing the prescribed strategy. Questions are answered such as: Who is going to talk to, or intervene with this person? What exactly will you say or What is the goal of intervention? When will the intervention take place? and To which advisor will the student report the results of the intervention?

The final phase is *follow-up*. Once the action plan has been formed and executed, follow-up takes place to insure that all went according to plan and to assess any further needs of those being rescued.

The final point on the agenda of a TOUCH meeting is to provide additional *training and education* for the members of the intervention team.

BRIDGING THE GAP

The analogy of a bridge will help you better understand the overall TOUCH helping process. The team is a "bridge" rather than the "destination" for the hurting person. The students who are part of the program are the "road" on that bridge, pointing troubled peers to the help they need. The advisors are the "rails." These advisors define the parameters of the bridge and keep the student helpers focused on their purpose: to bridge the gap between the hurting person and the help he or she needs. The "rails" prevent the "road" from straying from its focus to one side or another. Because the parts of the bridge must rely on each other to be effective, cooperation is imperative.

The Concept at Work
An intervention team advisor shared this story of how the TOUCH concept has worked:

> An intervention team member was sitting in a class and noticed another student doodling in his notebook. He could see inscriptions such as "I hate myself," "I wish I were dead" and some morbid drawings. During a TOUCH meeting, the team member brought his concern for this student to the group. Another team member mentioned that he had this same person in one of his classes. Others mentioned that they saw this person at different times during the day. The team decided to surround the student with comfort, encouragement and empathetic "ears."
>
> They learned through their efforts that he was struggling with some problems and was considering suicide. Because of their intervention, he was encouraged and worked through this crisis period.

We have seen hundreds of similar examples. This type of intervention would have never occurred had it not been for students who were involved in an intervention program. Most likely, this successful intervention effort would not have occurred if the team members had not been taught to be aggressive in caring for and helping others.

Perhaps the most touching portrait of this caring ethic at work comes from the testimony of a senior in high school who was on a TOUCH team. After I had participated in a follow-up TOUCH training session, Brian came up to me and told me about one of his experiences. A handsome, articulate and intelligent young man, Brian had been selected by his peers as someone they could talk to in troubled times.

He told me about going to the cafeteria one day and, as he was passing through the line, he noticed one of the school "loners" sitting at a far corner table. "I was walking with my tray to the familiar table where my friends sat," Brian shared, "but I couldn't take my eyes off that loner. I thought about how we had talked about reaching out to lonely people...just being friendly is enough to let them know you care.

"I could feel my friends' gazes on my back as I did something I had never done before. I walked to that far corner table and sat down and had lunch with the kid that everyone ignored. That's something I know I never would have done had I not gone through this training."

This was not a high-risk situation—not yet, anyway—but of all the testimonies I have heard from students who have helped other students, this one stands alone at the top. It vividly demonstrates that, first of all, involvement in such a program can affect a student's character and, secondly, that caring can become a priority in students' lives and make an impact in their world.

EIGHT

Administering Emotional First Aid

ALTHOUGH I cannot remember her name, I remember her pain. She kept her head bowed to the floor, trying to muffle the sobs coming from deep within her. I remember thinking, *Who would suspect that a sweet-looking girl like this is broken in spirit?* The girl had a delicate, childish face framed with soft brown curls—sort of like an adolescent Shirley Temple. Her words revealed preteen simplicity, but grown-up heartache.

"I just wish I could die," she whimpered through her sobs.

"What happened?" I asked.

"It's my mom," she volunteered, "she doesn't want me."

Because I had heard this same statement from many hurt-ing teenagers, I immediately pictured an angry, bitter, abusive mother telling her child to get out of her life and blaming her for all of her problems.

I asked, "Did she say she wanted you out of the house?"

"No," she responded.

I dug further, "Did she say she didn't want you?"

"Well...not exactly," she said.

"What exactly *did* she say?" I asked.

She whimpered, "She said...she said that I was an accident."

I almost wanted to chuckle, but I did not because I saw how emotionally distraught she was.

She continued, "I heard my parents say that all the other kids in my family were planned except for me. I don't think they ever really wanted me. And when my mom gets mad and yells at me, I think she wishes that I was never born. And then I just wish I was dead."

Amazing, I thought to myself, *this girl seems to come from a well-adjusted, functional family. She has given no evidence to the contrary.*

Other teenagers in the room had been kicked out of the house, abused physically and verbally, raped by stepfathers. Yet this girl was as emotionally shaken as any of them—over a statement that was probably spoken in lighthearted jest.

While growing up, I remember my parents often joking that three out of their five children were "surprises" (or "accidents," if you will). Although I knew my birth was not planned, I never once remember feeling unwanted.

I decided to take a poll of everyone in the room. I asked the 25 or so teenagers there, "How many of you have heard your parents say, jokingly or otherwise, that your birth was not planned?" About 13 of them raised their hands. In wide-eyed amazement, the girl looked at all of the raised hands—almost as if she had discovered some long-lost friends!

I turned to her and said, "My parents joked that I was an accident...it kind of makes me wonder. Here is one 'accident' (pointing to myself) trying to encourage another 'accident' (pointing to her). The logical conclusion is that this whole conversation must be an 'accident'—unless you believe like I do that God craftily used the carnal cravings of your parents to put you on this earth." The kids all had a good laugh at that. I added, "Sometimes even our parents are unwitting participants of God's purposes."

I then shared these thoughts with the group: "I've always thought it funny that people's 'accidents' somehow become part of God's plan. Whether your parents say jokingly or seriously that you never should have been born, there is Someone else who has a different opinion on the matter."

The girl who had been sharing looked at me wide-eyed, "You really think so?"

I nodded, "Yes."

An analysis of this situation reveals a number of observations. First of all, we see the fickleness and tenderness of a young adolescent's feelings. Secondly, we see the importance of making each child feel special and significant—especially among his or her peers or siblings.

While every good parent wants a child to have a positive sense of self-worth, children often interpret words and events in terms of preconceived ideas they have about themselves and how their parents feel about them. Consequently, it is essential that parents build relationships with their children that are characterized by openness and communication.

The most vulnerable time in parent/child relationships is during discipline. In these moments a teenager is apt to fall into a "persecution complex" or "unfavored child" line of reasoning. Contrary to the rhyme, "Sticks and stones may break my bones, but words can never hurt me," kids are significantly affected by parents' words—especially words of disapproval.

Compounding this problem is the difficult time parents have separating the crime from the criminal. Rather than dealing strictly with the child's negative behavior, parents often label the child with the negative behavior. For example, calling the child with a propensity toward sloppiness a "slob" or "pig" affirms in the child's mind that this is the picture the parent has of him. In his book, *Seeds of Greatness*, Denis Waitley discusses the importance of separating the performance from the performer:

> In communicating with others, always treat *behavior* and *performance* as being *distinctly separate* from the *personhood* and *character* of the individual you are trying to influence. Instead of saying, "Clean up your room, you pigs," say something like, "All of the bedrooms in our home are neat and clean. While you're cleaning up the room, I'll be at the store. When I get back, I'll show you a way to help separate your clothes better, in the closet."[1]

A negative label for a child is never appropriate. Such a negative label often becomes the prognostication of future behavior. For example, if children hear a negative label, they may begin to believe it, and then correspondingly align their lives with it.

SHARING CRITICISM

In all of our interpersonal relationships, there are some general guidelines for sharing criticism with others. First of all, I have found that my first response is usually my worst. I like to picture my mind as being a sort of "food processor" for words. If I respond before putting my thoughts through the "food processor," my words usually will be rough, blunt and difficult for the recipient to digest. If I first "process" my words, they will be shredded, softened and much more digestible for the individual receiving them.

Consider the following list of guidelines for sharing criticism with others:

1. Talk about behavior, not personality traits;
2. Be specific;
3. Be relevant;
4. While criticism should not always be shared on the spot, it should be shared as soon after the offense as possible;
5. Criticism should be given directly, not hinted at or communicated through a third party;
6. Give the other person a chance to explain;
7. Give it caringly;
8. Criticism is not constructive when hurt is the motive— then it becomes a form of attack;
9. As a general principle, do not nag or hound a person about his or her behavior unless the person has asked you for your input;
10. Avoid being judgmental;
11. We are not always required to deal with the "why" of a negative behavior, so avoid over-analyzing a behavior and just deal with what you see;
12. Learn to see between the lines and interpret what a person is saying; he may be talking about external circumstances but is actually trying to say he is hurting or afraid;
13. Share the positive—even under negative circumstances;
14. Avoid sarcasm or a condescending manner when sharing criticism;

15. Be subtle in giving advice so that you do not set yourself *above* the individual.

FOCUS ON THE REAL ISSUES

After dealing with hundreds of intensely frustrated people, I
have come to the conclusion that the predominant source of
their frustration is their focus on areas over which they have
no control. While we all desire to change or control the per-

---

**It is somewhat amusing to discover that the list of changes
teenagers felt they could make seems to be the ideal list
parents would draw up for them.**

---

son or situation that is causing us grief, most likely we cannot.
And although we have to live with this circumstance, we often
fantasize that we do not.

Whenever teenagers begin to talk about the issues in their
lives, they inevitably describe frustrating experiences. Their
focus, whether it be a parent, friend, situation or loss, seems
drawn to variables and circumstances over which they are
powerless. It is this sense of powerlessness that often leads an
individual toward a general lethargy and attitude of despondency. For example, suicidal logic reasons, "If I have no control, why should I bother to live? Suicide is the only area that
gives me any control. I can make the decision to end my life
and I will do it!"

Once again, suicide is *not* the issue here. The issue is that
person's perspective on his or her experiences. If that individual's perspective can be changed—or even altered slightly—

to introduce new light on the topic, the person will begin affecting realistic changes in their life. Their thoughts of suicide will begin to diminish.

When counseling young people, I avoid the temptation to tell them what to do and the haughty attitude exemplified by the words, "If I were you, I would...." Rather than making decisions for these young people, I guide them to their own conclusions. In the process, I help them focus more realistically on their problems. This enables them to develop a more positive perspective of their situation and discover those areas where they can take control of their lives.

Because a positive perspective is the goal of my counseling sessions, the word "suicide" never comes up and rarely are the words "drugs and alcohol" even mentioned. These negative alternatives for dealing with problems are out of place—and almost laughable—from a positive point of view. Let's take a look at how this process of guiding a young person from despair to hope can take place.

CAN YOU TELL ME HOW TO GET TO SERENITY STREET?

Most teenagers seem to feel that the best destination in life is "Excitement Alley" or "Popularity Place." What all people desire instinctively, however, is peace of mind. In workshops with teenagers, I describe the journey from "Sesame Street" to "Serenity Street" as long, bumpy and treacherous. And once they have arrived at "Serenity Street" life is not without its troubles.

The most successful guidance I have been able to offer troubled teenagers has been the simplest. Like the Alcoholics Anonymous reform model, this guidance revolves around the logic of the "Serenity Prayer."[2] The "Serenity Prayer" reads:

"God grant me the serenity to accept the things I cannot change, the courage to change the things I can, and the wisdom to know the difference." The two action words used here are *accept* and *change*.

Most of us have found that acceptance is the most elusive emotional skill. It is difficult to bring ourselves to cope with injustice, unfairness and pain. The logic of the "Serenity Prayer" helps teenagers learn this difficult but essential skill. To guide students in applying this logic to their lives, I begin by asking the two following questions:

1. What things in your life that you cannot change do you find hard to accept?
2. In what areas of your life can you realistically influence change?

Some of the insightful responses to the first question that I have received from the thousands of teenagers I have surveyed include:

- Their looks or general appearance;
- Their limitations, abilities, talents and capabilities;
- People (parents, friends and relatives);
- Uncontrollable circumstances;
- Loss (death, divorce, moving, etc.);
- The past mistakes they have made and the resulting feelings of regret, embarrassment, guilt and loss of confidence;
- Past harms that they have suffered and the accompanying emotions of anger, hurt, sadness, anxiety, guilt and bitterness.

The *changes* these teenagers feel they have a realistic possibility of affecting are:

- The development of certain abilities;
- Their values and priorities;
- Their attitudes and beliefs;
- Their goals;
- Their expectations;
- Their choice of friends;
- Their habits.

It is somewhat amusing to discover that the list of changes teenagers felt they could make seems to be the ideal list parents would draw up for them. This tells me two things: teenagers know what specific changes need to be made in their lives and they will not make those changes until they feel the need or see the benefit of doing so.

An exercise that has helped many teenagers identify what they can and can't change is what I call my "Serenity Street Worksheet" (see appendix for an example). On a blank sheet of 8 1/2 x 11-inch paper ask each teenager to draw a line dividing the page into two equal columns. At the top of the left column have each one write the word "Accept." At the top of the right column have each one write the word "Change."

Down the left side of the "Accept" column instruct each one to list categories that describe the things about life they cannot change: looks, limitations, people, uncontrollable circumstances, past mistakes, harm suffered. (Tell them to leave space between each thing they list.) Then encourage each one to think about his or her own life and the specific things described by each category listed that cause the most frustration.

After they have done this, have each one write these specific frustrations under the categories on the paper. For example, if the teenager has a parent that constantly "grinds" away at their state of serenity, have the teen write that person's name under the category "people" listed on the paper.

If the teenager's source of frustration is something about himself, have him write that frustration under the categories "looks," "limitations" or "uncontrollable circumstances." If there was an event in his childhood that traumatized or "zapped" his confidence, it should be written under the categories "past mistakes" or "harm suffered." Continue this process until each frustration has been listed appropriately.

In the "Change" column, instruct the teenagers to list categories that describe the areas of life where they can realistically affect change: abilities, values/priorities, attitudes/beliefs, goals, expectations, friends, habits. Again, have each individual think about specific frustrations described by the categories listed that he or she has experienced. Direct each one to write under the appropriate categories listed those specific frustrations he wants to change.

At this point the individual must decide whether or not to pray for the "serenity to accept the things I cannot change" and "the courage to change the things I can" and then to act accordingly. I think "the wisdom to know the difference" comes largely from the realization that his or her sphere of influence is restricted by what he or she can change and the action taken to affect those changes.

POSITIVE PROBLEM MANAGEMENT

The next step in administering emotional first aid is to help troubled teenagers solve their problems. As was highlighted in the Serenity Street approach, we cannot control the actions (circumstances and people) around us. But we can control our reaction. Rather than wasting time trying to change others' behavior or uncontrollable circumstances, we should concentrate on our responses to our circumstances and others' behavior. Once teenagers are able to identify their real problems, they are on the path toward solving or managing that problem and reconciling the situation.

Those of you who are in a position to influence teenagers know the challenge of helping them develop problem-solving skills. For this reason, I strongly advocate an approach that, when possible, puts the responsibility for cooperating and deciding on the action in the hands of the teenager. This

---

All too often, the young person tries to dismiss all of life as a "bum experience" when it is really his *current* problems that are piling up and seem too massive to manage.

---

approach also tends to be more effective because most people will follow a decision they have made on their own more than the advice of someone else. (Obviously, if a teenager is out of control and a threat to his or her own health and others, this rule does not apply.)

Counseling by Questions

To help teenagers come to their own conclusions, I guide them by using a series of questions. In this way I am perceived as an interested listener rather than a counselor. If they view me as a sort of "guru" or "answer man," then the bulk of the responsibility to fix the situation rests upon my shoulders. When I direct them with a "road of questions" they formulate their own answers.

Counseling by questions, as with any counseling method, is really subtle manipulation. Although the word "manipulation" often arouses negative responses, it has its positive functions. To manipulate something simply means to affect its motion or direction. Correspondingly, the goal in talking to a troubled teenager is to affect his or her motion and direction toward positive change.

I like to illustrate this approach for teenagers by using a card trick. I lead the teenagers through a series of questions manipulating them to choose a particular card which they believe they have chosen on their own. I then ask them if they think I can force their card to gravitate to the very bottom of the deck. Of course they are skeptical. I then ask them to look at the bottom card. To their amazement, they discover that their card *is* at the bottom of the deck. They become even more skeptical when I tell them that they had no choice but to choose that particular card. I explain that the card was at the bottom of the deck all along and that I simply manipulated them to name that particular card. This card trick illustrates that, by asking the right questions, you can influence a person to arrive at a predetermined destination in thought and at the same time allow him to feel in control of his own situation and decisions.

In counseling by questions, I first ask open-ended questions such as, "What has been bothering you the most?" or "What problems are causing you the most stress right now?" These kinds of questions allow you to lead a person to open up and share his or her feelings. Closed-ended questions such as, "Are you OK?" or "What's the matter?" often result in quick replies such as, "Yes" or "Nothing." Counseling by asking questions helps the person identify his or her specific problems. A leading question might result in a response like, "Life stinks!" You can now calculate your next leading question which might be something like, "What is its most recent odor?"

I have also learned that young persons can focus more realistically on their situation if any responses and feelings about what we are discussing are written down.

Breaking Down the Problem

All too often, the young person tries to dismiss all of life as a "bum experience" when it is really his *current* problems that are piling up and seem too massive to manage. This young person's perspective is like the man whose home was ravaged by a hurricane—he does not know where to begin the clean-up. By opening up and talking about his problems, each of the problems can be defined and separated from the others. At this point problems become more manageable and appropriate plans for dealing with them can be made.

Once this young person has separated his problems, they can be prioritized and the most significant or leading problem can be identified and discussed. I initiate this process by asking the question, "Who or what caused this problem?" I like this question better than, "Who or what do *you* think caused this problem?" The latter question may be perceived as, "Give me *your* inferior opinion about the problem and then I'll tell you the right opinion—what *I* think."

This provides an opportunity for the troubled and frustrated young person to vent his emotions. The worst thing a counselor can do at this point is disagree with, judge or analyze the person's response. Rather, let the person blame whomever and whatever he or she will. If the individual wants to attribute the source of his problems to Gadhafi, Communism or the greenhouse effect, that's fine! If this avenue of expression is not opened up, these emotions will surface later. Most likely they will interrupt the process of establishing his or her goals to affect change.

As the individual lays the blame for his own actions on another party or circumstance, each person or event should be explored. This is important because often the individual's sense of confusion and hopelessness evaporates simply by talking about his inner turmoil. Strategically posed questions can serve as a crucial catalyst toward relieving this emotional stress. Once the teenager has been able to air his negative feelings, you are ready for the next step in the process.

This step is initiated by asking questions such as, "Have you contributed in any way to the situation at hand?" or "Is there anything you might have done to make this situation worse for yourself?" Be careful to present this question in a tone of curiosity rather than of accusation. If the teenager senses that you are pointing an accusatory finger at him, the teenager's defense mechanisms will activate. This will probably cause him or her to retreat behind the walls of denial and self-justification. You will then be emotionally expelled to a comfortable distance. In any counseling situation you always want to convey the understanding that, "Right or wrong, I'm on your side." You do not want to project a superior attitude that says, "I am here to fix you."

Clearing the Path Toward Clarity
In considering the teenager's role in compounding the problems at hand, he will need to begin some self-analysis. This journey into self has been facilitated by clearing the path of obstacles: the role others may have played in creating the problems has been examined and this young person has had the opportunity to realize, "*I* am ultimately responsible for my own actions." I often tell young people that responsibility is having the ability to respond in a desired way.

Now the individual is usually ready to confess those things for which he or she feels at fault. The teenager might say, "Well, I have been pretty mean," "I've said some bad things," "I've tried to hurt some people," or "I've been out to show them a thing or two."

This will help you both realize that no matter how bad the young person might be feeling about what others have done or what has happened in the teen's life, the individual is feeling equally bad about his own response to the problem.

As we discovered in the Serenity Street approach, people have no control over the actions of others or, to a certain extent, the happenings of life. But people do have providential control over their own responses to these things.

When the young person discusses his faults or negative behavior, I just nod in interest. (Remember to encourage that person to write down his or her responses; this will help the person organize his feelings.)

Setting Goals, Resolving Problems

From this point the process of counseling, or guiding by asking questions, takes a positive turn toward setting goals to resolve the individual's problems. But the road to recovery and stabilization is an uphill climb. A desired destination cannot be reached by someone driving in neutral hoping to be pushed along. Teenagers need to realize that in order to reach the place where problems are resolved and goals are reached, they will have to shift their own life into gear.

To guide someone in setting goals that will resolve his problems I ask the question, "What could you do to improve this situation?" At this point, you want to keep the person in an introspective mode where he can consider a broad spectrum of possible solutions without committing himself to a specific action. The question, "What *could* you do?" (rather than "What *will* you do?") gives the individual the freedom to survey all the possibilities.

If the individual does not take time to ponder all the options before deciding on the action he will take, it is unlikely that the person will complete that action. The reason for this is that, prior to making a commitment to change, a person must be convinced he is making the *best* possible decision.

When asking the question, "What could you do?" point specifically to some of the causes of the problem the individual has identified (refer to any causes he may have written down). Ask, "What could you do about this particular situation?" "What could you do about this relationship?" or "What could you do about your response to this situation?" Even if the answer is "nothing," at least now the individual will see his limitations and the futility of trying to affect change in those areas.

The solution for many problems is often the flip side of the cause. For example, if one of the causes of a young person's negative behavior is the influence of negative companions, then an obvious part of the solution would be to find new, more positive companions. Or, if a major component of the problem is the person's inability to control his temper, then part of the solution is for that person to find positive ways to express angry feelings and control outbursts.

I want to interject at this stage that, although you are guiding the direction of this process, the individual should feel that he is finding his own answers.

Commitment for Change

After the individual has surveyed the possibilities, it is time to ask the pivotal question, "What *will* you do?" I often state this question in the following way: "Out of all of the options you have listed for yourself (note that I use the word "you" rather than "I" or "we"), which ones do you think you will have to do?"

It is here that the individual is equipped to make a commitment for change. In helping a person plan his action, I use what I call my "Positive Problem Management Form" (see appendix). On this form I first direct the person to list the change he or she wants to make. Then I direct him to list the steps involved in making that change.

It is in planning the steps the person will take that many counseling sessions fail. Too often counselors focus their energy on trying to get people to commit themselves to making a change but never assist them in specifically defining the necessary steps to cause that change.

I remember talking to one girl who was having a great deal of difficulty at work. When it came time for her to commit to making a change, the first thing she said was, "I am going to get a new job."

I asked her, "What kind of job?"

She quickly replied, "I don't know."

Then I asked her, "How are you going to get a job?"

Once again she answered, "I don't know."

If we had not discussed her chosen course of action further, I wonder what her chances would have been for getting a new job. In this girl's case, I helped her develop a detailed list of steps that would help her find another job. First we realistically surveyed her abilities and marketability. Then she made a list of options such as reading the want ads, going to see an employment counselor, making an appointment with someone who could help her write a resume, and writing a resume.

To help her come up with these options I asked her, "What help do you need to get this done?" This kind of question helps people begin to understand what it really takes to make it in this world. Sometimes this means accepting help from others, education or training in specific areas and/or physical, psychological, social or spiritual development.

After the girl had listed what steps she would take and what help she would need, I helped her set a deadline by which to accomplish her goal.

In guiding individuals through this process of problem management, I have seen some amazing transformations take place. For example, when I first began talking with the girl I described above, she was confused, disorganized and misdirected. By the time we had completed the process she had a realistic plan by which she could affect change in her life—step by step. She could confidently say, "Hey, I can do it. I'm not stupid. I'm back in control." To be back "in control" was what she needed (and is what every troubled human being strives for).

WITHOUT LOVE, YOUR EFFORTS ARE USELESS

What I have offered in this chapter are tools that will help you competently deal with troubled teenagers. What I cannot give you is a capacity for compassion and empathy. In order to be effective, you must compassionately communicate to teenagers that they are lovable and worthy, despite their behavior or situation. This process of administering emotional first aid in the hands of an apathetic counselor is useless.

One grieving girl who had just lost her boyfriend to suicide told me, "I don't want to talk to any counselor."

"Why?" I asked.

"Because, when my boyfriend died, I was taken to a psychiatrist. The entire session he thumbed through a textbook while he asked me questions. He never once made eye contact with me. And I noticed on a form, when the session was ending, that he had written down a psychological label for me."

This girl was disillusioned with the adult helping process. The person who was given the opportunity to help her deal with her pain did not even care enough to make eye contact with her. She did not need a label—she needed love. If all she needed was a label, they should have taken her to a packing plant. There simply is no replacement for T.L.C. Expressing love and support is emotional first aid at its best!

Notes

1. Denis Waitley, *Seeds of Greatness: The Ten Best Kept Secrets of Total Success* (Old Tappan, NJ: Fleming H. Revell, 1983), p. 33.
2. "The Serenity Prayer" was written by Dr. Reinhold Niebuhr (1892-1971) in 1943 for a service in the Congregational church of Heath, Massachusetts, where Dr. Niebuhr spent many summers. The prayer was first printed in a monthly bulletin of the Federal Council of Churches. Enormously popular, it has been circulated in millions of copies. The popular version quoted here differs only slightly from the original version.

NiNE
For Those Left Behind

JULIE and Scott were having a fight—a fight not unlike any other misunderstanding between high school sweethearts. Julie was visibly upset. Fighting back tears, she was trying to keep her resolve about ending a relationship that had grown rather destructive.

Julie liked Scott. He was a fun-loving guy who wore a big smile and seemed to have a cheery word or comment for everyone at school. He drove the most impressive truck of anyone in his class. Cruising in this incredible truck gave one the impression of being elevated 20 feet in the air! And in this rural community a boy stood about as high as his truck.

Sometimes Scott complained that girls only wanted to be seen in that bold, pitch black truck to impress their friends. But Scott knew this was not the case with Julie. She always sat right next to him, eyes fixed upon his winning grin, oblivious to the sometimes jealous onlookers.

However, Julie had a difficult time dealing with the dark, melancholic side of Scott's personality. Scott often became gloomy, overly introspective and negative. Without meaning to, he often took it out on Julie. He had so many questions about himself: "If I am so popular, why am I so unhappy?" "What am I going to do with my life?" or "Why can't people like me for me?"

The night of the argument, Scott and Julie were at Scott's home. Julie had made it very clear that she needed a break from the emotional roller-coaster ride that characterized their relationship. Not surprisingly, Scott did not react well to this news.

Scott smelled heavily of alcohol—some sort of whiskey or other hard liquor. Julie assumed from his slurred words, emotional instability and irrational manner that he was drunk.

After arguing heatedly, Scott angrily made his exit. As he ascended the stairs he yelled, "I swear...if you break up with me now...I'll...kill myself!"

As he disappeared around the corner Julie yelled back, "Don't talk like that!"

Then it came. The sickening blast rang out, a deafening sound to Julie's ears. It jolted her into a surreal, almost dreamlike state. "I didn't hear that...he didn't...*Oh, my God....Scott!...Scott!*"

But there was no answer.

Running to the top of the stairs, Julie found Scott laying motionless on the floor. A blank, confused expression was on the part of his face that was left. The top part of his head had been blown off and the walls were covered with blood. Julie frantically tried to put his head back together—almost as if she were performing first aid.

Julie began pleading, "You're going to be okay, Scott. Just don't stop breathing. Please hang on until I can get you back together...until we can get you to the hospital...Scott!"

But there was no life left in Scott. He had died instantly as the bullet went through his brain.

The ambulance crew arrived quickly in response to a neighbor's call after hearing the shot. A crowd began forming outside the house. When the paramedics entered the home, they found Julie sobbing, cradling Scott's head.

Julie told her story in one of my high school rap sessions. After talking to the student body at this particular school, 57 students gathered in a room wanting to share their problems. Julie was one of them.

The students' faces appeared forlorn and strained. I knew they had not come to skip a class or waste time. There had been a number of suicides in this community and I knew this group represented many of the teenage survivors.

I glanced at the clock—it was already 2:00 P.M. There was not enough time to deal with their problems in anything more than a superficial manner. I sensed that an unstable volcanic reserve of grief was about to burst at any moment. I knew I needed more time in order to deal effectively with these troubled lives.

"I know all of you need to talk," I stated. "But there's no way we can deal with the issues facing 57 people in an hour and a half."

"I think you should talk to the school about setting aside more time for you to spend here," suggested one student.

A desperate-looking 16-year-old girl begged, "We *need* to talk to someone!"

The atmosphere was charged with unrest. The students were anxious to deal with their needs and the general consensus was that the administration would not agree to disturb another day of learning.

I told them I would talk to the administration about arranging meetings with them the following day. The principal was more than willing to help. I spent the entire next day working with small groups of students, helping these survivors put their lives back together.

Because these young people had lost a number of friends to suicide, they were confused, guilt-ridden and desperate for some inward peace. None of them, save Julie, had gotten any help. No one in the community had addressed the issues that a survivor of suicide faces. When a person loses a friend or family member to suicide, he or she needs some therapy—whether it be short-term or long-term. If these issues are not properly addressed and dealt with, they will mushroom and burden the survivor for the rest of his or her life.

The only reason Julie went to see a professional was because her parents insisted. (Julie was the girl I mentioned in the previous chapter whose visit to a psychiatrist was a negative experience.) This time Julie did find help by talking with a small group.

Julie had been literally tormented day and night with the thought that she had driven Scott to suicide. Under the circumstances, who could blame her for thinking that way?

As Julie was sharing her story with the group, another girl told Julie something she had never heard before: "Julie, two years ago I was going out with Scott. One night I found him sitting all alone in a dark room playing with a gun."

Others also shared with Julie what they knew of Scott's destructive behavior in the years and months before his suicide. The pieces of the puzzle began to fall slowly into place as each shared what they knew about Scott. Julie listened with wide-eyed amazement. So, it had not been her fault. She was only Scott's most recent scapegoat.

Scott had been struggling long before Julie had ever met him. Scott took his own life. No one helped him. No one else pulled the trigger. And no one had even faintly encouraged him to do so. Scott had lived in a lonely, dark world by himself. Because he had kept his struggles to himself, none of his friends had been able to help him.

But because of Scott's decision to end his own life, each of his friends was now struggling to understand life. Because of their association with Scott, most of them were experiencing pain. Julie had been crippled and it was going to take a miracle of healing—emotionally and psychologically—to restore her. Fortunately we had witnessed the first glimmer of hope for her.

As intensely sad as Julie's story is, it is but one of millions. For each of the approximately 30,000 suicides reported per year in the United States, it is estimated that there are at least five to ten intimate survivors who must deal with serious grief issues. Unless these hurting individuals get some help, they may never experience healing. Even with help the survivors must still live with the reality that a loved one took his or her own life.

The issues survivors of suicide face go beyond those of the "normal" grieving and mourning process. Suicide survivors often blame themselves, believing they should or should not have said or done something. The survivor often feels responsible for the person's death, even though the individuals know they did not pull the trigger, force down the pills or tie the noose. It often takes years to fight through the intricate web of guilt felt by those left behind by suicide.

SURVIVAL HINTS

Following are some of the survival hints I share with those left behind by suicide. This information has been written largely by suicide survivors.

"What ifs" and "If onlys" unmercifully torment survivors day and night. They wonder, "What if I had called the doctor sooner?" "What if I hadn't let him or her take the car tonight?" or "What if I had only taken time to listen?" They also blame themselves by saying, "If only I hadn't gotten mad" or "If only I'd expressed my love better." These thoughts only create a vicious, unending cycle of tortuous suffering—and the questions always remain unanswered.

Although feelings of guilt are normal when a loved one dies, these feelings are often unrealistic. There is a tendency to blame oneself for contributing to the loved one's death. Guilt, an already strong emotion, often becomes magnified because the bereaved is extremely vulnerable.

Guilt is often experienced when a survivor of suicide tries to answer why his or her loved one died. One dictionary defines guilt as the "fact or state of having done wrong or being to blame."[1] This implies a connection between guilt, sin and the ability to cope. To be guilty of something bad is to be responsible for it.

As we are well aware, none of us can live close to a person without hurting or experiencing hurt. We all do and say things that we later regret. Therefore, when a loved one commits suicide, the survivors are plagued by agonizingly painful memories of those hurts, whether real or imagined. We then consider every possible action we could have taken or should not have taken to prevent this death.

It is normal for grieving people to feel some degree of guilt, but these feelings can be *real* or *excessive*. Real guilt is the result of destructive things we intentionally do to hurt one another. Real guilt is the desire to make up for past mistakes. We may also feel remorse because of wasted opportunities within a relationship. All too often it is not until a loved one has died that we experience guilt for lost opportunities and all the things we neglected to do.

It is helpful to emphasize for survivors of suicide that they probably did the best they could under the circumstances. Had they known more, they would have done more.

Excessive guilt, on the other hand, shoulders all the blame and responsibility for a loved one's death. Excessive guilt unrealistically assumes that had we not done this or that our loved one would be alive. The implication is that the survivor often subconsciously sees him- or herself as powerful enough to have saved the life of the deceased.

If a person is experiencing excessive or prolonged grief, he needs professional help to work through his feelings. It is helpful to emphasize for survivors of suicide that they probably did the best they could under the circumstances. Had they known more, they would have done more. In his book, *When Bad Things Happen to Good People*, Rabbi Kushner suggests,

> An appropriate sense of guilt makes people try to be better. But an excessive sense of guilt, a tendency to blame ourselves for things which are clearly not our fault, robs us of our self-esteem, and perhaps, of our capacity to grow and act.[2]

Usually, guilt is not satisfied by explanations. Survivors often feel helpless to deal with their guilt because little can be done to correct the situation. Because of the loved one's death, the direct contact the survivors want with the deceased in order to deal with their guilt is impossible to arrange.

The bereaved may find some relief by talking about their feelings of guilt to a trusted friend. An understanding friend can be a means by which these feelings can be verbalized and dealt with. It is important for survivors to find a friend who will listen and accept their feelings without being judgmental. When well-meaning friends tell a person not to feel guilty, they are not being helpful.

If feelings of guilt are unmercifully tormenting a grieving person, it is important to recognize those feelings. By ignoring or repressing one's feelings, guilt is only intensified. A person's feelings are never wrong, even though at times they may be based on unrealistic or distorted perceptions. Because feelings help us understand the impact of an event upon our lives, it is vitally important to pay attention to these feelings. By first accepting our feelings, we can begin the process of finding forgiveness. Forgiveness is the key for dealing with feelings of guilt.

Although the loved one has died, the bereaved can still ask that person for forgiveness. There will be no response, but it is the asking that is important. This asking allows the guilt-ridden to consciously release his or her guilt. It is helpful to realize that had we been asked to forgive a loved one, we would have.

Finding forgiveness begins with the decision to seek and accept forgiveness when it is offered. In his book, *Living When a Loved One Has Died*, Earl Grollman quotes a clergyman who said, "I believe that God forgives you. The question is: Will you forgive yourself?"[3] Someone else tells of a friend who asked a survivor, "How many times have you asked God to forgive you?" The reply was, "Hundreds and hundreds." The friend responded, "Too bad you wasted so much time. God forgave you the first time you asked." This realization (that God has forgiven you) opens wide the door for forgiving oneself.

By accepting God's forgiveness, people can begin to forgive and love themselves. Then they can be healed of their guilt. Both Judeo-Christian teaching and psychology stress the importance of accepting and offering forgiveness in order to maintain inner health. Without forgiveness feelings of guilt will only deepen and harden.

Therefore, for guilt to be dealt with in a healthy manner it must be acknowledged, accepted and forgiven. This process may take great effort, but the results are worth it. Otherwise, over a period of time, guilt may lead to years of unhappiness and/or psychosomatic illness.

Grief over the loss of a loved one is painful enough in itself. It does not help the survivor of suicide to add to his or her grief unwarranted blame or accusations. No one can change the past. The grieving survivor must deal with real feelings of guilt and at the same time cultivate hope. Furthermore, the bereaved must realize that excessive, unrealistic grief cannot be worked out. It must be released.

And, finally, the survivor must learn to forgive the deceased for the action he took. I believe Jesus' words, "If anyone of you is without sin, let him be the first to throw a stone" (John 8:7), are just as applicable when the offender is deceased.

SUGGESTIONS FOR HANDLING GUILT

These suggestions offer, in a nutshell, advice for those who feel burdened by guilt.

1. If you do feel guilty, admit it to yourself as well as to others who will listen and care.

2. Remember that you are human, not perfect. There are many things that you may have tried to do and yet failed. There may also be things that you simply could have done and did not. Accepting your imperfections will aid you in working through your guilt.

3. Realize that living involves experiencing both good and bad.

4. If you feel guilty, ask yourself what things bother you the most. Talk over your feelings of guilt with a trusted friend or professional and confess your guilt to God.

5. Talk honestly about why you feel guilty. This will help you separate real guilt from excessive, unwarranted guilt.

6. Forgive yourself for those things for which you are really guilty. Ask for forgiveness from God and those you have hurt.

7. Release your feelings of guilt for those things that are not your fault.

8. Try to realize that what happened is past. There is nothing you can do now to change what has happened.

9. Determine to live life to the best of your ability.

10. What you learn from your guilt will help other people in your life. If necessary, adopt a new life-style in the future. Your past mistakes may help you change for the better.

11. Realize that sometimes you are powerless; you cannot control everything that happens.

12. Realize that guilt is a normal part of grief and should ease with time.

13. If guilt is hindering your recovery, seek professional counseling. Don't be afraid or embarrassed to talk about your feelings of guilt with those who have been trained to help.

14. Remember the special times that you had with the loved one who has died.
15. Consider that your loved one would probably not want you to continue to suffer from guilt and grief.
16. Remember there is not always an answer for "why" questions. You do not have to find someone (yourself) or something to blame for your loved one's death.
17. Be patient with yourself. Remember that you tried to do the best you could to help your loved one with what you knew at the time.
18. If your faith is shaken, try to put your beliefs back together and find comfort in God.
19. Try writing down your thoughts/feelings of guilt.
20. Allow your family and friends to comfort you and show love to you.
21. Establish some purpose or meaning in your own life by focusing on helping others. Volunteer to help with some charitable organization or support group. By helping others you will help yourself.
22. Try not to blame yourself for things that you did not know you were mishandling.

Along with feelings of guilt, the suicide survivor is plagued by feelings of shock, denial, loneliness and anger. The grief process for survivors of suicide can also contain an extremely painful element of confusion. This is why survivors are often consumed with the search for answers to questions such as: Why did this person have to die? For what exact reason did he or she die?

It is extremely difficult to isolate the cause for a suicide. If it is possible to perform a "psychological autopsy" on the deceased, you may be able to pinpoint several things that motivated their self-destructive act. More than likely, you will find not one single factor, but an emotional avalanche of negative stimuli: failed relationships, external pressures and internal frustrations.

Any person who is trying to support a suicide survivor will benefit from information that deals specifically with suicide grief. The National Suicide Help Center offers a *Survivors of Suicide*[4] packet that deals with grief issues such as helping the family grieve, surviving holidays, living through a child's suicide, surviving the loss of a sibling and helping children through grief.

MANAGING THE AFTERMATH

Ironically, the day I was writing this chapter I received a phone call from a high school. A 15-year-old girl who attended there had just committed suicide. The counselor was calling to see if I could come and talk to the students. Not surprisingly, the entire student body was in a state of emotional upheaval. I discovered that the suicide had come on the heels of another 15-year-old who had died of natural causes.

I learned that the students were responding to this situation by expressing a fear to make friends because of the possibility they might somehow lose them. In addition to this trauma, drug and alcohol abuse among the students was rising significantly.

Over the phone I sensed a tension and urgency in the counselor's voice. I quickly suggested that two things be initiated. First, we would need to begin talking realistically to students about life and its "hard to swallow" realities. The students needed to understand that life is not always good, but often painful. Because we cannot control many circumstances and what others do, we often have to live with things we dislike.

Secondly, we needed to begin talking with students about

how to deal with life. To do this we would need to help the students answer questions such as: How will you begin to sort out your feelings? If you have suffered loss, you are experiencing grief. How does grief affect people and where are you in the grief process? or Are you dealing with reality or are you trying to change things which are beyond your sphere of con-

---

As much as we hope it will never happen to us, the fact remains that tragedy gives us no notice.

---

trol? Are you unconsciously trying to undo what has happened? Are you taking steps to help yourself? Do you have a solid support system? Who will you turn to share your feelings? or What habits and coping mechanisms do you use to deal with pain and stress?

These questions constitute what I call a "Reality Survey." If an individual can comfortably and honestly answer these questions, they are ready to face reality and find healing. If an individual cannot come to grips with the answers to these questions, they will most likely slip into a ditch of escapism such as drugs and alcohol.

PREPARING A "POSTVENTION" PLAN

Schools, churches and other community organizations need to be prepared for a suicide crisis. As much as we hope it will never happen to us, the fact remains that tragedy gives us no notice. If we are not prepared ahead of time, we will frantically scramble around when a crisis hits—like ants around a trampled anthill.

Following is a "postvention" (after-the-suicide) plan that

will help you act effectively if such a tragedy occurs. Although this plan is worded for application to a school setting, the concepts apply to a church or any other organization that works with teenagers.

I. Preplanning
   A. Decide in advance who will be in charge of directing the postvention plan following a suicide. Designate a substitute in the event that the appointed person is unavailable at the time of the emergency. Make certain that all staff members know who these people are.
   B. At least once a year provide thorough training on suicide prevention for teachers in every high school and junior high school.
   C. Provide training for school secretaries on how to handle telephone calls and requests for information from the community.
   D. Use phone trees to communicate as rapidly as possible with persons who need to be informed and involved in enacting the postvention plan.

II. The school principal should be informed immediately of the suicide. (The principal should contact those necessary to begin enacting the postvention plan. The aid of school resource staff may be enlisted in order to plan and implement the school's response).
   A. Collect factual information about the suicide.
   B. Prepare a written statement about the suicide.
   C. Make arrangements to respond to the needs of staff and students who were close to the student who committed suicide.

    D. Notify the staff of a meeting to be held as soon as reasonably possible.

III. Staff Meeting
    A. Inform the staff of the suicide and review the facts in order to dispel any rumors.
    B. Provide teachers with a written announcement to be read during the first class of the day.
    C. Announce any special arrangements made to respond to the needs of staff and students.
    D. Encourage the staff to discuss the incident with the students as needed to dispel rumors. Discourage "glorification" of the event in order to minimize any contagious responses by students.
    E. Encourage the staff to handle student expressions of grief or loss to the extent that they are comfortable. Students who are distraught or express a need to talk should be referred to the identified resource staff.

IV. Carry out and monitor the activities set forth above.

V. Follow up with affected students.
    A. Prioritize your response to and follow-up with affected students according to the following three categories:
       1. Intimate survivor;
       2. Peripheral survivor;
       3. A similar type personality (may not have been close to the deceased, but would relate to him or her on the basis of personality style and interests—if a loner commits suicide, otherloners within the school are apt to be affected by it).
    B. Interview all those suspected of being at risk to

assess their risk level (refer to chapter 6 for help in assessing and responding to a student's risk level).
C. Make recommendations to survivors and their families as to the best therapy for their situation.

In an effort to downplay the suicide, many schools overreact by "squelching" information and responses—to the point of impeding the grief process of the students. For example, after a suicide some schools will not allow grieving students to go to the funeral because they don't want to "glamorize" the suicide. By not treating a suicide like any other death and by not allowing students to grieve the loss of a friend and classmate, the school has done what I call "backdoor glamorization." Not only are they hindering the grief process, but they are subtly condemning the deceased. As a result, they have glamorized and sensationalized the suicide even more.

Other issues that must be dealt with in a school setting are questions such as: What will we do with the empty desk in the classroom? What about the deceased's locker? or What if the deceased played on a team, was in the band or part of the theater group? How will those teammates express their grief?

It would be impossible to outline in detail the steps to follow in reference to these questions. I will suggest, however, that each teacher or group leader allow the surviving teenagers to discuss possible answers. Doing this will help you uncover what they feel would be appropriate expressions of mourning. For example, to hastily remove the empty desk could communicate insensitivity on the part of the teacher. On the other hand, to leave the empty desk there too long could prolong the grief process beyond reasonable limits. The students can provide you with insight to help address these questions in a healthy, constructive way.

SOMEBODY OUT THERE IS HURTING

For some unexplained reason, when Dave was 15 years old, he became the object of persecution and torment. It is hard to explain why the verbal bullies pick the targets they do. Although the experiences of any age are no worse than adolescence, for some reason it seems to be a "make-it-or-break-it" period for self-esteem.

Dave was a good-looking, intelligent and personable guy. Nevertheless, other guys in the school had taken it upon themselves to make him as miserable as possible. Just when it seemed like the persecution would never end, Dave's reprieve came—a new kid in school. The new boy, Jeff, was an easy target. Aside from being a new face in the crowd, Jeff was not real bright and he didn't have the look of someone destined for possibility.

Ironically, Jeff was assigned to Dave as part of a buddy system to help him become oriented to the school. As Dave took Jeff on his rounds, he watched the bully contingency turn their venomous affections toward Jeff. As bad as he felt for Jeff, Dave almost relished the opportunity to be off the hook.

Years later Dave told me, "For the first time, I had some peace of mind. I used to hate going to school because I knew what I would face each day. But not anymore. Now it was Jeff's turn.

"Jeff had a lot of problems, both at home and at school. It was so strange...here I was supposed to be his buddy, and yet I used him as buffer from all the persecution I used to get. And I enjoyed the relief. I could have told the guys to shut up and leave him alone. I could have stuck up for him...but I didn't...but I didn't..." his voice trailed off.

"And then one day I came to school and found out that Jeff had put a gun under his chin and shot himself in the head. I can't describe the guilt and pain I felt. But I can tell you that Jeff's death led me to an intense period of suicide contemplation. No one knew I was thinking about it but it was staring me in the face everyday."

Dave made it through that nightmarish time in his life because he had found support and help. Today, Dave is active in leadership on his college campus. He is doing what he can to help other students who might be troubled.

There are a lot of "Daves" out there. Sometimes their parents haven't a clue what they're thinking. Sometimes even their closest friends are not aware of the turmoil they are enduring. The same burden of responsibility that Dave felt for Jeff's death is carried by many every day. For some, guilt wraps itself so tightly around their necks that it squeezes the very life out of them. While there is nothing we can do about those that have already ended their lives, there *is* a great deal we can do to reach those who have been left behind.

> So many tears have fallen
> Many more are on the way.
> We can't be sure, but wasn't death
> Too high a price to pay?[5]

Notes
1. *Webster's Third New International Dictionary* (Springfield, MA: Merriam-Webster Inc., 1971), p. 1010.
2. Harold S. Kushner, *When Bad Things Happen to Good People* (New York: Schocken Books, 1981), p. 94.
3. Earl Grollman, *Living When a Loved One Has Died* (Boston: Beacon Press, 1977), p. 41.
4. *Survivors of Suicide* (Rochester, MN: National Suicide Help Center, 1987).
5. Anonymous. Written by a 17-year-old survivor.

Epilogue

I am sure many of the people mentioned in this book are still searching. They are searching for answers, peace and hope. Some answers they will never find. Peace of heart and mind and hope for the future may still be eluding them. This is an empty and frustrating feeling.

I know that frustration and emptiness. When I was 17 years old and got down off that bridge rail late in the night, I knew my search was just beginning. The only answer I found that night was that suicide was not the answer. However, this insight did nothing to make life easier. If anything, it made life more difficult. I was now caught between not being able to enjoy life and not being able to kill myself. I needed something...and I did not know where to start looking.

My search led me to philosophical, mystical and metaphysical books. Many of them titillated my imagination but inevitably left me with my internal emptiness.

Later that year I went backpacking in the Big Horn Mountains of Wyoming. I went as a chaperone for a YMCA trip for seven delinquent youths. One day, we all got lost by taking the wrong fork in the road. Angry and flustered I turned back and started running. I ran until my strength gave out. By now I was at least a mile ahead of everyone else. Then it happened—the strangest, yet the most real experience of my life.

I was panting for breath in the thin mountain air. I was as tired outside as I was inside. Suddenly, I felt surrounded by a Presence. It was foreign to me but I felt perfectly comfortable. Gentle but peaceful thoughts were coming to me. I felt I was in a conversation with someone I could not see.

You can't make it alone.

I began to choke up.

You need Me in your life.

Warm tears began to slide down my face. My tears felt so good—for it had been so long. Something began to break within me.

Open your heart to me.

I heard myself say words I could not recall ever having heard before. Somehow, instinctively, I knew who This was.

I pleaded, "Jesus, help me! Take my life. I give my heart to you."

Everything broke loose within me. I sobbed harder than I ever had and felt cleansed with every passing moment. It was all leaving me—the pain, the anger, the confusion, the hopelessness.

I felt brand new inside. I felt loved, forgiven and truly grateful to be alive. I felt peace—what indescribable peace. I experienced a total internal calm and contentment. I sang to Him songs that heretofore had meant nothing...but now were as if I wrote them. I talked to Him. I ran. I jumped. I smiled so hard I thought my face would break.

I made a deal with Him. I said that I would meet Him the next day at the same time to see if He was really real or if this was my imagination. I showed up the next day. So did He.

I left that mountain inspired. I, for the first time, had purpose in my life. From that point on, I knew that my life would mean something.

Thank you Jesus for meeting me up there.

I hope some of the people mentioned in this book and others like them will meet You too.

Appendix

Building the Bridges...

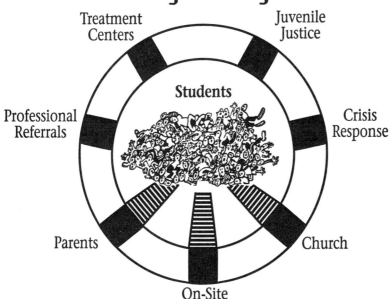

Treatment Centers

Juvenile Justice

Professional Referrals

Crisis Response

Parents

Church

On-Site

Students

Circle of Prevention

...Between the Hurting and the Helping

The Numbers
90/100 to peers
10/100 to adults
50 percent get help
50/100 troubled teens do not get help

Can You Tell Me How to Get to Serenity Street?

ACCEPT (Past, People and Uncontrollable Circumstances)	CHANGE (Ideas, Attitudes, Companions and Controllable Circumstances)

Counseling and Guiding by Questions
Leading into Serenity Street

A wise person once said, "Be wary of giving advice, wise men don't need it and fools don't heed it." Given the fact that most people are predisposed to deflecting advice, it is not a wise practice to give it out unless requested. Even when requested, it is still best to let the seekers find their own answers as they are more likely to act upon their own conclusions. The "Counseling by Questions" format has been written to aid in the process of helping an individual come to his own conclusion about what direction to take. If troubled persons are misdirected, this format easily and inoffensively redirects them (or better helps them to redirect themselves).

I. Lead Question:

    A. Options:

        1. *What* is the problem?
        2. *What* is bothering you?
        3. *Why* are you upset?

B. Rather than: Faults:

  1. Are you OK?   * Close ended
  2. Is anything wrong?   * Opportunity to evade

Let the person define the problem in his own terms, no matter what those terms may be. Your job is *not* to set him straight or to judge.

II. Question Two:

What/who caused this problem?

This is the individual's chance to blame, accuse, and vent his frustration/anger. The individual may not yet be ready to admit his role in creating trouble. The troubled person needs the opportunity to air out personal feelings.

III. Question Three:

A. Options:

  1. What *might* you have done to make things worse?
  2. What things have you done that might have worsened the situation?
  3. Have you responded in a way that has made things worse for yourself or others?

This gives the individual an opportunity to admit his role in heightening or escalating the problem or crisis. Now we begin to lead into solutions rather than just dwelling on the problem.

IV. Question Four: (Possibilities/Brainstorming)

What could you possibly do to help this situation?

Anything goes here. The individual needs to look at all of the possibilities. At this point it is not necessary that any solutions be reached; instead, the various options must be considered. Suggestions can be given in the form of a question such as: What do you think of the idea of _____? Be careful to affirm all good ideas. Important Note: See "Serenity Street" guide at this point to keep the process on the right track.

V. Question Five: (ACTION!)

What *will* you do?
What *are* you going to do?

We have now reached the moment of truth. It is commitment time. If the individual wants to receive help, it will be displayed here. However, if the individual is not ready, this will be apparent as well. If the individual is apathetic at this point, we can simply say, "When you are ready to work things out, I would sure like to help in any way I can." This type of statement reveals: (1) We can't do for the individual what he will not do for himself; and (2) We are not "dropping the individual overboard." We still care about the individual and are making ourselves available when he does decide to act. On the other hand, if the individual states his plan of action, we should affirm it and offer our assistance in any way possible.

VI. Final Question: (Setting a date with Destiny)
   When are you going to _____?

Studies show that we accomplish 90 percent more when we write down our goal and set a date to accomplish it. Nothing motivates us quite like a deadline. We need deadlines for our own good. Goals are only vague possibilities until we commit to *when* it will be accomplished.

VII. Follow-up:

Once an individual commits to a specific time of action, we then commit to immediately getting back in touch to see how things went. At this time, we can add further encouragement. REMEMBER! Nothing helps a troubled person more than the feeling received from coming up with his own answers and taking steps in his own behalf. Often what we do for the troubled person can actually work against success. The individual needs to see that he *can* reach a solution.

Positive Problem Management Form

I. Problem:

II. Causes:

   Exterior (Outside factors that have caused the problem.)

   1.

   2.

   3.

   4.

   Interior (Things I've done to make it worse.)

   1.

   2.

3.

4.

III. Positive Options Available

What could I do to improve my situation?

1.

2.

3.

4.

5.

6.

7.

8.

9.

10.

IV. Changes to be made: These things I will do.

1.

2.

3.

4.

5.

Change #1—Steps	Change #2—Steps	Change #3—Steps
1.	1.	1.
2.	2.	2.
3.	3.	3.
4.	4.	4.
5.	5.	5.
6.	6.	6.
7.	7.	7.
8.	8.	8.
9.	9.	9.

V. Resources Needed

Whose help and what things will I need to make these changes?

1.

2.

3.

VI. Steps to take for completion

1.

2.

3.

4.

5.

ANTHONY'S LAW—
IF SOMETHING CAN GO RIGHT IT WILL.

THE survivors of suicide I have mentioned will tell you that they know there is nothing they can do to bring back their friend or loved one. They will also tell you that there is plenty we all can do to keep suicide from happening in the first place. The organizations I work with—**The National Suicide Help Center** and **Teens in TOUCH**—exist for this purpose.

The National Suicide Help Center offers suicide prevention training courses in written, audio and video formats. The Center also acts as a consultant for those seeking to establish prevention centers and survivor support groups.

Teens in TOUCH is dedicated to educating teenagers and those who work with teenagers about providing care and support for hurting friends. Teenagers must be armed with the necessary information if they are going to effectively help their friends. This needed information is shared through talks to teenagers, training workshops for teenage groups interested in helping their peers and by establishing programs where teenagers help their peers find purpose in life.

Both of these organizations can be reached by writing to:

P.O. Box 34, Rochester MN, 55903
and by calling (507) 282-2723.